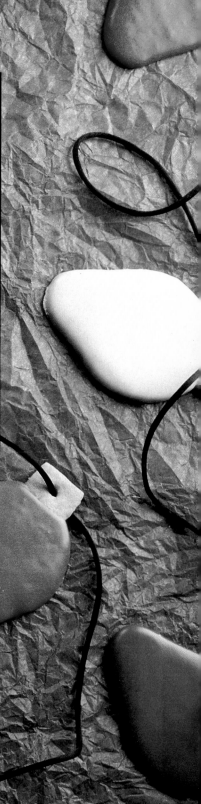

Christmas GIFTS OF GOOD TASTE

*S*urprising family and friends with well-chosen gifts is one of the great joys of Christmas. And when those gifts are treats from the kitchen and handmade crafts from the heart, they give pleasure that can't be found in any store. Through them, we're able to bestow uniquely personal presents while enjoying the wonderful satisfaction that comes from creating them. And because of the loving effort involved, we share a little bit of ourselves through the handmade offerings we present to those we love.

Christmas Gifts of Good Taste *was written to help you add that loving touch to all your Yuletide gift-giving. It's brimming with delicious recipes and charming craft ideas developed especially for Christmas. There's sure to be something in this book to delight everyone on your gift list. May it bring special joy to your Christmas celebration!*

Anne Childs

LEISURE ARTS, INC.
Little Rock, Arkansas

Christmas GIFTS OF GOOD TASTE

EDITORIAL STAFF

Editor: Anne Van Wagner Childs
Executive Director: Sandra Graham Case
Creative Art Director: Gloria Bearden
Executive Editor: Susan Frantz Wiles

PRODUCTION
Managing Editor: Sherry Taylor O'Connor
Foods Editor: Susan Warren Reeves, R.D.
Crafts Designer: Patricia Wallenfang Sowers
Technical Writers: Kathy R. Bradley and
  Dawn R. Kelliher
Production Assistants: Diana Heien Suttle and
  Nancy L. Taylor
Test Kitchen Assistant: Nora Faye Womack

EDITORIAL
Associate Editor: Dorothy Latimer Johnson
Senior Editorial Writer: Linda L. Trimble
Editorial Writers: Laurie R. Burleson and Marjorie
  Lacy Bishop
Advertising and Direct Mail Senior Copywriter:
  Eva M. Sargent

ART
Production Art Director: Melinda Stout
Senior Production Artist: Linda Lovette
Art Production Assistant: Cindy A. Zimmerebner-
  Johnson
Photography Stylist: Karen Smart Hall
Typesetters: Cindy Lumpkin and Stephanie Cordero
Advertising and Direct Mail Artists: Sondra Harrison
  Daniel and Kathleen Murphy

BUSINESS STAFF

Publisher: Steve Patterson
Controller: Tom Siebenmorgen
Retail Sales Director: Richard Tignor
Retail Marketing Director: Pam Stebbins
Retail Customer Services Director: Margaret Sweetin
Marketing Manager: Russ Barnett

Executive Director of Marketing and Circulation:
  Guy A. Crossley
Fulfillment Manager: Scott Sharpe
Print Production: Nancy Reddick Lister and
  Laura Lockhart

Table of Contents

Table of Contents

Table of Contents

A⁺ APPLE DUMPLING

APPLE DUMPLINGS

2¼ cups all-purpose flour
½ teaspoon salt
⅔ cup plus 2 tablespoons butter or margarine, divided
6 tablespoons cold water
¼ cup finely chopped pecans
¼ cup granulated sugar
1 teaspoon ground cinnamon
4 large Granny Smith apples, peeled and cored
1 egg white
4 1-inch cinnamon sticks
Green food coloring

Preheat oven to 400 degrees. In a large bowl, combine flour and salt. Using a pastry blender or 2 knives, cut in ⅔ cup butter until mixture resembles coarse meal. Sprinkle water over; knead until a soft dough forms. On a lightly floured surface, use a floured rolling pin to roll out dough to a 16 x 17-inch rectangle. Use a sharp knife to cut out four 8-inch squares. Cut out 8 leaf shapes from dough scraps.

In a small bowl, combine next 3 ingredients; stir until well blended. Place an apple in center of each square of dough. Place about 1 tablespoon sugar mixture and about 1 teaspoon butter in center of each apple. Brush egg white on edges of pastry and bring corners to top of apple, tucking corners into core of apple. Arrange 2 leaves on top of each pastry-covered apple. Insert cinnamon stick in top of pastry. Stir food coloring into remaining egg white and brush on leaves. Transfer to a greased 8-inch square baking pan. Bake 35 to 40 minutes or until brown. Store in an airtight container. Give with instructions for serving.

Apple dumplings may be served warm or at room temperature. To reheat, preheat oven to 350 degrees. Bake uncovered on an ungreased baking sheet 5 to 8 minutes or until heated through.

Yield: 4 apple dumplings

APPLE BASKETS

For each basket, you will need an approx. 5½" x 5" x 6½" basket with handle (we used a 1-quart till basket), a 6" x 24" piece of fabric for trim and bow, a 13½" square of fabric for liner, hot glue gun, and glue sticks.

1. For trim on basket rim, measure width of rim and add 1"; measure circumference of rim and add 2". Cut a strip of fabric the determined measurements. Press edges ½" to wrong side. Overlapping ends, glue trim to rim.
2. For bow, cut a 2⅝" x 7" strip and a ¾" x 1¼" strip from fabric.
3. Press long edges of 2⅝" wide strip ½" to wrong side. With right side out, fold strip to form a loop as shown in Fig. 1.

Fig. 1

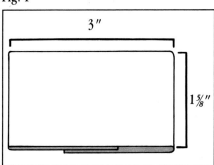

4. Press long edges of ¾" wide strip ¼" to wrong side. With right side out, wrap small strip around center of loop to form a bow; glue ends at back to secure. Glue bow to basket handle.
5. For liner, fringe edges of fabric square ⅜".

MAMA KRINGLE'S PIZZA

*M*ama mia! This Holiday Cookie Pizza delivers a scrumptious melding of flavors that's sure to satisfy any sweet tooth! Moist and rich, the giant treat has a buttery cookie crust topped with crunchy pecans, chewy coconut, and yummy chocolate chips. To present your Yuletide delivery, decorate a pizza box with the image of Mama Kringle, Kris's favorite baker.

HOLIDAY COOKIE PIZZA

CRUST

- ¼ cup butter or margarine, softened
- ¼ cup butter-flavored shortening
- ¾ cup firmly packed brown sugar
- 1 egg
- 1 teaspoon vanilla extract
- 1 cup all-purpose flour

TOPPING

- 1 cup (6 ounces) semisweet chocolate chips
- 1 cup finely chopped pecans
- ¾ cup sweetened shredded coconut, divided
- 1 can (14 ounces) sweetened condensed milk
- ½ cup Nestlé Treasures™ Premier Semi-Sweet Chocolate Deluxe Baking Pieces

Preheat oven to 350 degrees. For crust, cream butter, shortening, and sugar in a large bowl until fluffy. Add egg and vanilla; beat until smooth. Stir in flour; knead until a soft dough forms. Press dough into bottom and ½ inch up sides of a greased 12-inch round pan.

For topping, sprinkle chocolate chips and pecans evenly over crust. Sprinkle ½ cup coconut evenly over. Pour condensed milk evenly over. Bake 25 to 30 minutes or until crust is golden brown. While cookie is still warm, place chocolate pieces on top. Sprinkle remaining coconut evenly over. Cool completely in pan. Store in an airtight container.

Yield: about 16 servings

MAMA KRINGLE'S PIZZA BOX

You will need a purchased pizza carry-out box (our brown cardboard box measures 13½" x 13½" x 2");
craft paper; 12" squares of white, green, and black paper; tracing paper; graphite transfer paper; black felt-tip pen with fine point; peach, pink, dk pink, red, blue, lt green, green, and grey colored pencils; spray adhesive; ¾"h white vinyl stick-on letters (available at craft or art supply stores); 1½"w craft ribbon; and craft glue.

1. (*Note:* Use spray adhesive for all gluing unless otherwise indicated.) Use box lid as a pattern and cut a piece from craft paper; glue paper to lid.
2. Cut an 11" dia. circle from black paper. Center and glue circle to lid.
3. Cut a 10¾" dia. circle from green paper; cut an 8½" dia. circle from center of 10¾" dia. circle and discard. Center and glue green ring to black circle.
4. Cut an 8¼" dia. circle from white paper. Trace Mama Kringle pattern onto tracing paper. Use transfer paper to transfer design to center of white circle. Use pen to draw over outlines of design. Use colored pencils to color design. Center and glue white circle to black circle.
5. Use stick-on letters to write the following on green paper ring: MAMA KRINGLE'S PIZZERIA and A TASTE ''YULE'' LOVE.
6. Use craft glue to glue ribbon to sides of box.

CARDAMOM CANES

*F*oretell a sweet Noel for a friend with a basket of candy cane-shaped rolls! Baked in this festive form, our delicious Cardamom Bread Twists are brushed with a light coffee glaze. The quick-to-make bread cloth, with its Yuletide proverb, adds an extra dash of holiday cheer. For a playful touch, tie some of the "candy canes" with colorful ribbon.

CARDAMOM BREAD TWISTS

- 3¼ cups milk
- ½ cup butter or margarine, softened
- 2 cups granulated sugar, divided
- 3 eggs
- 2 teaspoons ground cardamom
- 1½ teaspoons salt
- 3 packages quick-rising dry yeast
- ½ cup warm water
- 12 cups all-purpose flour
- 1 cup hot brewed coffee

In a medium saucepan, bring milk to a boil; remove from heat and cool to room temperature. In a very large mixing bowl, cream butter and 1½ cups sugar until fluffy. Add next 3 ingredients, mixing until smooth. Dissolve yeast in water. Add milk and yeast mixture to creamed mixture; mix until well blended. Add flour 2 cups at a time, mixing thoroughly after each addition.

Preheat oven to 350 degrees. On a lightly floured surface, knead dough until soft and pliable. Use a floured rolling pin to roll out dough to ½-inch thickness. Cut dough into 1 x 9-inch strips. Twist 2 strips together into a candy cane shape and transfer to an ungreased baking sheet. Repeat with remaining strips of dough. For glaze, dissolve remaining sugar in coffee; set aside. Bake bread 30 minutes; brush with glaze. Bake 5 to 10 minutes longer or until golden brown. Store in an airtight container.

Yield: about 2½ dozen bread twists

BREAD CLOTH

You will need desired size square of unbleached muslin fabric, ruler, and red permanent felt-tip pen with fine point.

1. Fringe edges of muslin ⅜".
2. With bottoms of letters ¾" from edges of muslin, use pen to write "These Shapes Foretell A Sweet Noel" along 2 edges of muslin.
3. Draw dots and dashes ¾" from edges of muslin.

A Bright Surprise

These Christmas Light Cookies will be a bright surprise for your special friends. Imagine how their faces will light up when they discover what's packed inside the cleverly disguised gift box! The mint-flavored treats are easy to make and fun to decorate with icing in traditional tree light colors.

Christmas Light Cookies

COOKIES

- ¾ cup butter or margarine, softened
- ⅓ cup granulated sugar
- ⅓ cup firmly packed brown sugar
- 1 egg
- 1 teaspoon mint extract
- 2 cups all-purpose flour
- ¾ teaspoon baking soda
- ⅓ cup finely ground walnuts

ICING

- 5 cups confectioners sugar
- ½ cup plus 1 tablespoon milk
  Green, red, orange, and blue paste food coloring

For cookies, cream butter and sugars in a large bowl until fluffy. Add egg and mint extract, beating until smooth. In another large bowl, sift together flour and baking soda. Stir flour mixture and nuts into creamed mixture, mixing until a soft dough forms. Cover and chill 1 hour.

Preheat oven to 350 degrees. On a lightly floured surface, use a floured rolling pin to roll out dough to ¼-inch thickness. For pattern, follow Transferring Patterns, page 122. Place pattern on dough and use a sharp knife to cut out cookies. Transfer to a greased baking sheet. Use a drinking straw to make a hole at the bottom of each cookie. Bake 8 to 10 minutes or until cookies are light brown. Cool completely on a wire rack.

For icing, beat sugar and milk in a large bowl until smooth. Divide icing evenly into 5 small bowls. Leaving 1 bowl white, tint remaining bowls green, red, orange, and blue. Referring to photo, spread icing on cookies. Allow icing to harden. Store in an airtight container.

Yield: about 2 dozen cookies

Christmas Lights Box

You will need a box with lid, brown craft paper, transparent tape, white paper, red paper, desired lettering stencil, stencil brush, paper towels, removable tape (optional), black acrylic paint, rubber cement, and tissue paper to line box.

1. Follow Gift Box 1 instructions, page 123, to cover box with craft paper.
2. For box label, follow Step 2 of How To Stencil, page 122, to stencil ''CHRISTMAS LIGHTS'' on white paper. Cut label desired size.
3. Cut a piece of red paper ¼" larger on all sides than label. Center label on red paper; use rubber cement to secure.
4. Position label on box; use rubber cement to secure.
5. Line box with tissue paper.

ENCHANTING ELF BASKET

Who could resist goodies delivered in this enchanting elf basket! For a merry gift that's sure to warm up any holiday gathering, tuck a jar of spicy Beer Mustard into his lap with some pretzels and a stick of sausage. The friendly fellow will continue to delight your friends long after the treats are gone.

BEER MUSTARD

- 1 bottle (12 ounces) dark beer
- 2 cups dry mustard
- 1 cup firmly packed brown sugar
- 2 teaspoons salt
- ½ teaspoon ground turmeric
- 2 tablespoons apple cider vinegar
- 2 tablespoons dried minced onions

Pour beer into a small bowl, cover loosely, and let stand at room temperature overnight. Whisk beer and remaining ingredients together in a large saucepan over medium-high heat. Bring to a boil, whisking constantly. Remove from heat; cool to room temperature. Store in an airtight container in refrigerator. Serve with pretzels and sausage.

Yield: about 2 cups mustard

ELF BASKET

You will need 1 approx. 8″ dia. basket, two 9″ x 20″ pieces of unbleached muslin fabric for elf body, one 2¾″ x 17″ piece of fabric for legs, one 9″ x 20″ piece of fabric for tunic, one 4″ x 22″ torn strip of fabric for scarf, two 6″ x 10″ pieces of fabric for hat, four 6″ squares of fabric for boots, one 2″ square of burlap for hair, 1⅓ yds of cotton string, tracing paper, fabric marking pencil, small crochet hook (for turning fabric), graphite transfer paper, seam ripper, one ½″ dia. jingle bell, two ⅜″ dia. jingle bells, thread to match fabrics, polyester fiberfill, fabric glue, hot glue gun, glue sticks, one ⅜″ dia. shank button for nose, black and red permanent felt-tip pens with fine points, and powder blush.

1. Use body pattern, page 14, and follow Transferring Patterns and Sewing Shapes, page 122, to make body from muslin pieces. For ears, machine stitch along dotted lines. Trace face pattern onto tracing paper. Use transfer paper to transfer face to body. Stuff body with fiberfill. Sew final closure by hand.

2. Draw over face and ear detail lines with black pen. Color tongue with red pen. Apply blush to cheeks. Hot glue button to face for nose.

3. For tunic, fringe short edges of fabric ¼″. Matching right sides, fold fabric in half lengthwise. Use a ½″ seam allowance and sew long edges together. Press seam open. For neck opening, use seam ripper to rip a 5″ opening along center of seam. Baste around opening ¼″ from pressed edge. Turn right side out.

4. Place tunic on body. Pull basting thread, gathering fabric around neck. Knot and trim ends of thread.

5. Tie scarf fabric strip around neck.

6. For hat, trace hat pattern, page 14, onto tracing paper and cut out. Leaving curved edge open, follow Sewing Shapes, page 122, to make hat from hat fabric pieces. Press curved edge ¼″ to wrong side; use fabric glue to secure.

Tack ½″ dia. jingle bell to point of hat.

7. For hair, fringe 2 adjacent edges of burlap 1″. Hot glue burlap to top left side of head. Hot glue hat to head, covering solid portion of burlap.

8. For legs, match right sides and fold legs fabric piece in half lengthwise. Use a ¼″ seam allowance and sew long edges together. Turn legs piece right side out and stuff with fiberfill.

9. For boots, trace boot pattern, page 14, onto tracing paper and cut out. Leaving top edges open, follow Sewing Shapes, page 122, to make 2 boots from boot fabric squares. Press top edges ¼″ to wrong side; use fabric glue to secure. Tack one ⅜″ dia. jingle bell to point of each boot. Stuff bottom half of each boot with fiberfill.

10. Place 2″ of 1 end of legs piece into 1 boot; use hot glue to secure. Repeat to attach remaining boot.

11. Cut four 12″ lengths from string. Tie 1 length into a bow around each sleeve and boot.

12. Hot glue body to top of basket; hot glue legs around bottom of basket.

Continued on page 14

ELF BASKET (continued)

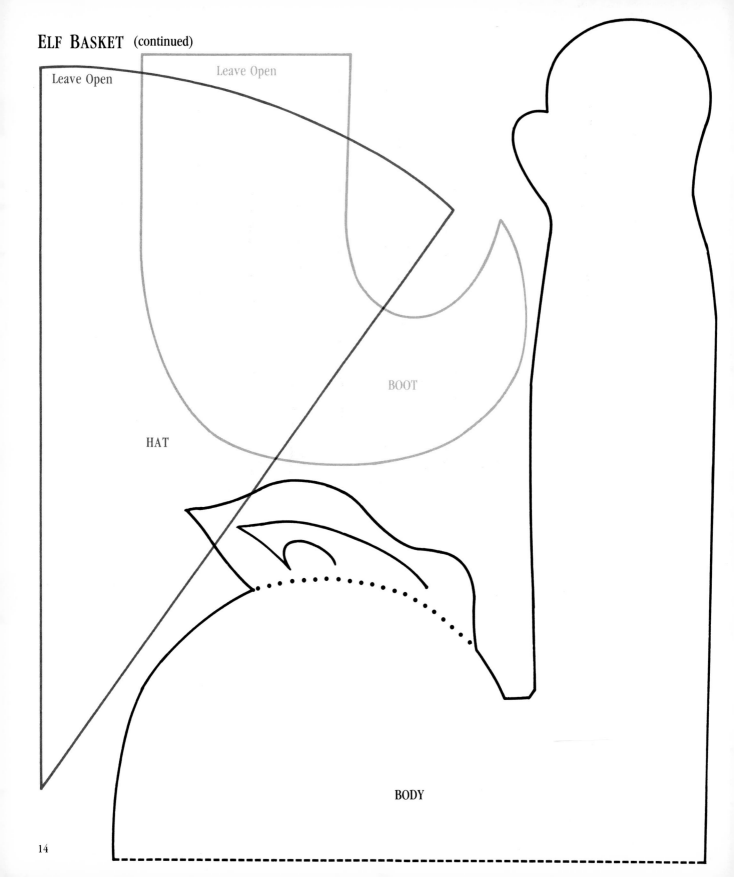

Leave Open

Leave Open

BOOT

HAT

BODY

FRUITY HOLIDAY TOPPING

*O*ranges, kiwis, and cherries make a colorful showing in this Marinated Fruit Medley. Great for spooning over ice cream or cake, the mixture gets its deliciously different taste from orange liqueur and anise seed. The cute no-sew stocking cap on our gift jar is easy to make from an ordinary red crew sock.

MARINATED FRUIT MEDLEY

    5 small oranges, peeled, seeded,
        and sliced
    2 kiwis, peeled and sliced
    1 jar (6 ounces) maraschino
        cherries, drained
    1 cup orange-flavored liqueur
    1 teaspoon anise seed
   ½ cup granulated sugar

Combine all ingredients in a large bowl. Stir until sugar dissolves. Cover and chill 8 hours or overnight to allow flavors to blend. Store in an airtight container in refrigerator. Serve alone or with ice cream or shortcake.

Yield: about 3 cups fruit

STOCKING CAP JAR TOPPER

For a topper to fit a regular canning jar, you will need a women's crew-style sock, a cotton ball or small piece of polyester fiberfill, 8″ of ⅛″w ribbon, and a ½″ dia. jingle bell.

1. Place cotton ball inside toe of sock.

Knot ribbon around sock just above cotton ball. Thread jingle bell onto 1 ribbon end; tie ribbon ends into a bow.
2. Fold cuff in half; fold in half again. Place cap over jar lid.

SANTA COOKIE CANISTER

Lightly sweetened with brown sugar, these unique Cashew Cookies are sure to please! Chopped cashews and cream cheese give the cookies a mild, nutty flavor. The easy-to-craft Santa canister makes a cute box for delivering the cookies and for holding holiday goodies throughout the Christmas season.

CASHEW COOKIES

- ½ cup butter or margarine, softened
- ¾ cup firmly packed brown sugar
- 4 ounces (½ of 8-ounce package) cream cheese, softened
- 1 egg
- 2 tablespoons milk
- 1 teaspoon vanilla extract
- 2 cups all-purpose flour
- ¾ teaspoon baking powder
- ¾ teaspoon baking soda
- ¼ teaspoon salt
- 1½ cups lightly salted chopped cashews

Preheat oven to 350 degrees. In a large bowl, cream butter, sugar, and cream cheese until fluffy. Add next 3 ingredients; mix until smooth. In another large bowl, sift together next 4 ingredients. Add dry ingredients to creamed mixture; stir until a soft dough forms. Fold in cashews. Shape dough into 1-inch balls. Transfer to a greased baking sheet. Bake 10 to 12 minutes or until light brown. Cool completely on a wire rack. Store in an airtight container.

Yield: about 5 dozen cookies

SANTA COOKIE CANISTER

You will need one 7″h x 6″ dia. Shaker box, one 1¼″ dia. drawer pull with screw, one 8″ long unbleached cotton craft mop (available at craft stores), fabric stiffener, two ½″ dia. black shank buttons for eyes, one 1″ dia. burgundy shank button for nose, hot glue gun, glue sticks, cream and burgundy acrylic paint, foam brushes, waxed paper, and matte clear acrylic spray.

1. Paint top of lid burgundy; allow to dry. Paint side of lid and drawer pull cream; allow to dry.
2. Center drawer pull on lid and attach with screw.
3. Spray outside of box and lid with acrylic spray; allow to dry.
4. For beard, trim mop to 4″ long and discard ends. Dip mop in fabric stiffener; squeeze to remove excess. With fabric tape at top of mop positioned horizontally and placed flat on work surface, place mop on waxed paper. Spread strands of mop into a fan shape. For each side of mustache, separate approximately 50 strands from each side at top of mop without exposing fabric tape underneath. Twist each side of mustache and trim ends even; allow to dry.
5. Remove beard from waxed paper. Curving beard to fit box, glue beard to box. Glue button over mustache for nose; glue buttons to box for eyes.

FOR A BREAD LOVER

*H*omemade bread straight from the oven is a special treat, and these Honey-Cheese Rolls are particularly good. A combination of Cheddar cheese and golden honey gives the yeast rolls a wonderful mild flavor. To delight a bread lover, deliver the rolls in the baking pan for easy reheating.

HONEY-CHEESE ROLLS

8 cups all-purpose flour, divided
2 teaspoons salt
2 packages active dry yeast
¾ cup butter or margarine, divided
2 cups (8 ounces) grated Cheddar cheese
1½ cups milk
⅓ cup honey
3 eggs

In a large bowl, combine 6 cups flour, salt, and yeast; stir until well blended. In a medium saucepan, combine ½ cup butter and next 3 ingredients. Cook over medium heat until a thermometer registers 130 degrees (butter may not be completely melted). Add eggs and cheese mixture alternately to dry ingredients, mixing until a soft dough forms. Gradually stir in remaining flour. Turn dough onto a lightly floured surface; knead about 10 minutes or until dough becomes soft and elastic. Transfer to a large greased bowl. Melt remaining butter in a small saucepan over low heat. Brush top of dough with ½ of melted butter and cover. Let rise in a warm place (80 to 85 degrees) 1 hour or until doubled in size.

Turn dough onto a lightly floured surface and punch down. Shape dough into 3-inch balls and place with sides touching in greased round 9-inch cake pans. If necessary, remelt remaining butter. Brush tops of rolls with melted butter and cover. Let rise about 1 hour or until doubled in size.

Preheat oven to 375 degrees. Bake 30 to 35 minutes or until golden brown. Cool completely in pan. Store in an airtight container. Give rolls with instructions for reheating.

To reheat, preheat oven to 350 degrees. Bake rolls uncovered 3 to 5 minutes or until heated through.

Yield: about 2 dozen rolls

WARMEST REGARDS

Our thick and spicy Hot Pepper Ketchup will give a friend a taste of the wild West! Flavored with a zesty combination of hot pepper sauce, garlic, chives, and celery salt, the tasty condiment will add gusto to hamburgers, hot dogs, and other fare. This hot pepper cowboy, crafted from papier mâché, cleverly disguises the ketchup bottle. His shiny silver badge conveys your "warmest regards," and the sprig of holly on his hat lends a Christmasy touch!

HOT PEPPER KETCHUP

1 can (12 ounces) tomato paste
½ cup vegetable oil
¼ cup tomato sauce
2 tablespoons chopped chives
1 tablespoon hot pepper sauce
1 tablespoon garlic powder
1 teaspoon celery salt

Whisk all ingredients together in a large bowl. Cover and chill 8 hours or overnight to allow flavors to blend. Store in an airtight container in refrigerator.

Yield: about 2 cups ketchup

HOT PEPPER COWBOY

For cowboy, you will need an empty 14 oz. glass ketchup bottle with cap, a 3½" x 9" piece of acetate (available at craft or art supply stores), masking tape, aluminum foil, instant papier mâché (we used Celluclay® Instant Papier Mâché), a craft stick, gesso, red acrylic paint, dk brown waterbase stain, foam brushes, a soft cloth, matte clear acrylic spray, a 4"w black felt cowboy hat (available at craft stores), 4" of ⅛"w silver braid, artificial holly sprig, and craft glue.

For tag, you will need a 3½"w wooden star cutout (available at craft stores), silver spray paint, black permanent felt-tip pen with fine point, and a black paint marker with fine point.

1. With 1 long edge even with bottom edge of bottle, wrap acetate snugly around side of bottle, overlapping short edges; tape to secure.

2. Leaving bottom of acetate tube open, wrap and crush pieces of foil around tube, forming a ¼" thick layer; continue wrapping and crushing foil around bottle to within 1" of top of bottle.

3. For chin, wrap and crush pieces of foil firmly around bottom of bottle, forming a 2" long pointed chin (Fig. 1). Pepper shape should be well shaped and firm before papier mâché is added.

Fig. 1

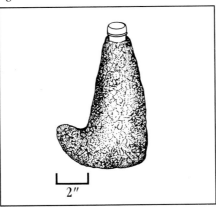

2"

4. Follow Papier Mâché instructions, page 122, to apply papier mâché over foil shape.

5. For nose, form a ¾" dia. roll of papier mâché 2" long. With 1 end (top) of roll 3½" from top of bottle, smooth top end of roll onto face. For nostrils, form two ½" dia. balls of papier mâché. Position 1 ball on each side of nose ½" from end of nose. Smooth balls onto face.

6. Use point of a pencil to make holes in papier mâché for eyes. Use eraser end of pencil to make holes for nostrils.

7. Use craft stick to form indentations on face for chin wrinkles and mouth.

8. Apply 1 coat of gesso and 2 coats of red paint to pepper, allowing to dry between coats.

9. Apply stain to pepper; remove excess with soft cloth. Allow to dry. Apply 1 coat of acrylic spray to pepper. Allow to dry.

10. Glue braid around crown of hat. Glue holly sprig to hat. Allow to dry.

11. Remove bottle from papier mâché pepper and fill with ketchup. Replace bottle in pepper and place hat over top of bottle.

12. For tag, spray paint star silver; allow to dry. Use paint marker to paint "WARMEST REGARDS" on star; allow to dry. Use pen to draw dots and dashes along edge of star.

MONOGRAM COOKIES

*O*ur Monogram
Cookies are great when you
need lots of special little
gifts for friends! Made with
nutritious graham flour,
the cookies have a rich
maple flavor. Lettering
stencils are used to personalize
the cookies and matching
gift bags. For a festive
touch, line the bags with
colorful fabrics.

MONOGRAM COOKIES

¾ cup butter or margarine,
    softened
⅔ cup granulated sugar
1 egg
1 teaspoon maple extract
2¼ cups whole wheat graham
    flour
¼ teaspoon salt

In a large bowl, cream butter and
sugar until fluffy. Add egg and maple
extract, beating until smooth. In another
large bowl, sift together flour and salt.
Stir dry ingredients into creamed
mixture, mixing until a soft dough
forms. Cover and chill 1 hour.

Preheat oven to 350 degrees. On a
lightly floured surface, use a floured
rolling pin to roll out dough to ¼-inch
thickness. Cut dough into 2½ x 3-inch
rectangles. Transfer cookies to a greased
baking sheet. Center a 2-inch lettering
stencil on cookie. Use a toothpick to
prick holes about ⅛-inch apart along
openings of stencil. Bake 12 to
15 minutes or until light brown. Cool

completely on a wire rack. Store in an
airtight container.

Yield: about 1½ dozen cookies

MONOGRAM GIFT BAGS

For each bag, you will need a small
brown paper bag, cream-colored
drawing paper, hole punch, desired
yarn, 1 button, craft glue, desired
lettering stencil (we used a 2″h Roman
stencil), red acrylic paint, stencil brush,
paper towels, removable tape (optional),
black felt-tip pen with fine point, and a
torn fabric square to line bag.

1. Follow Step 2 of How To Stencil,
page 122, to stencil desired letter on
paper. Use pen to draw dots around
edges of letter.
2. Trim paper around letter to desired
size. Glue letter to bag.
3. For tag, cut out tag shape; punch hole
at point. Write name on tag.
4. Knot 2 lengths of yarn around bag;
trim yarn ends 6″ from knot. Thread tag
onto yarn ends; tie ends into a bow.
Glue button to bow.
5. Line bag with fabric square.

SAUCY GIFTS

These versatile condiments make saucy gifts! Perfect for fondues, the Creamy Tarragon and Sweet and Sour Sauces are great for dipping shrimp or chunks of chicken and beef. The flavorful sauces may also be served on the side or added to casseroles for extra flavor. For a cheerful presentation, dress up the jars with handwritten labels backed with Christmasy craft ribbon.

CREAMY TARRAGON SAUCE

> 1/4 cup butter or margarine
> 1 tablespoon all-purpose flour
> 1 cup milk
> 1/2 cup sour cream
> 1 teaspoon dried tarragon
> 1 teaspoon dried chervil
> 1 teaspoon dried basil
> 1 teaspoon garlic powder
> 1/2 teaspoon salt
> 1/2 teaspoon ground black pepper

Melt butter in a medium saucepan over medium heat; stir in flour. Cook 1 to 2 minutes or until flour is brown. Gradually add milk; stir until flour mixture dissolves. Continue to cook, stirring constantly, until sauce thickens. Stir in remaining ingredients. Store in an airtight container in refrigerator. Give with instructions for serving.

To serve, transfer sauce to a medium saucepan. Cook over medium heat 3 to 5 minutes or until heated through, stirring occasionally. Serve warm with meat.

Yield: about 1 1/2 cups sauce

SWEET AND SOUR SAUCE

> 2 cups dry sherry
> 6 tablespoons honey
> 6 tablespoons red wine vinegar
> 2 tablespoons soy sauce
> 8 cloves garlic, minced
> 1/2 teaspoon salt
> 2 tablespoons cornstarch
> 1/4 cup water

Boil sherry in a medium saucepan over medium heat 10 to 12 minutes. Whisk in next 5 ingredients; remove from heat. In a small bowl, combine cornstarch and water to make a paste. Return sauce to heat; whisk in cornstarch mixture. Cook 3 to 5 minutes or until sauce thickens. Store in an airtight container in refrigerator. Give with instructions for serving.

To serve, transfer sauce to a medium saucepan. Cook over medium heat 3 to 5 minutes or until heated through, stirring occasionally. Serve warm with meat.

Yield: about 1 1/2 cups sauce

ORANGE CAKE

CAKE

- ¾ cup butter or margarine, softened
- 1½ cups granulated sugar
- 1 tablespoon grated dried orange peel
- 3 eggs
- 2½ cups all-purpose flour
- 2½ teaspoons baking powder
- ¾ teaspoon salt
- 1 cup milk
- 2 tablespoons frozen orange juice concentrate, thawed

ICING

- 4 cups confectioners sugar, divided
- 6 tablespoons milk, divided
- Red paste food coloring

Preheat oven to 325 degrees. For cake, cream butter, sugar, and orange peel in a large bowl until fluffy. Add eggs 1 at a time, beating well after each addition. In another large bowl, sift together next 3 ingredients. Stir dry ingredients alternately with milk and orange juice concentrate into creamed mixture, beating until smooth after each addition. Pour batter into 2 greased and floured 8-inch square baking pans. Bake 35 to 40 minutes or until a toothpick inserted in center comes out clean. Cool in pans 10 minutes. Turn onto a wire rack to cool completely.

For icing, combine 2 cups confectioners sugar and 3 tablespoons milk in a medium bowl; beat until smooth. Spread icing on sides and top of each cake. Allow icing to harden. To transfer pattern to top of each cake, trace pattern onto tracing paper. Center pattern on top of each cake and use a toothpick to punch holes about ¼-inch apart through pattern into icing. Remove pattern. Combine remaining sugar and milk in another medium bowl, beating until smooth. Tint with food coloring. Spread icing inside house design. Allow icing to harden. Store in an airtight container.

Yield: 2 cakes

This delicious Orange Cake decorated with a homey motif is the perfect way to show your neighbors how much you appreciate them. A popular old quilt pattern inspired the house design, which is easily created with Christmas-red icing. Our recipe makes two of the delicately flavored cakes so you can share this festive holiday greeting with more than one family!

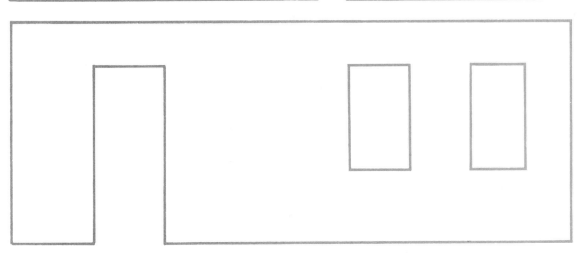

SNIP-AND-SNACK WREATH

A friend who's hosting a holiday gathering will be delighted to receive this snip-and-snack popcorn wreath. Using the scissors attached to the wreath, guests simply snip off the Granola-Coconut Popcorn Balls for a yummy snack. Loaded with healthy ingredients, this treat is a taste-tempting variation of the traditional recipe. What a fun addition to a Yuletide celebration!

GRANOLA-COCONUT POPCORN BALLS

- 1 cup granola cereal
- 1 cup sweetened shredded coconut
- 3 cups popped corn
- ½ cup firmly packed brown sugar
- ½ cup light corn syrup
- ¼ cup butter or margarine
- ½ cup smooth peanut butter

Combine first 3 ingredients in a large bowl. In a medium saucepan, combine next 3 ingredients over medium-low heat, stirring constantly until sugar dissolves. Attach candy thermometer to pan, making sure thermometer does not touch bottom of pan. Increase heat to medium and bring to a boil. Do not stir while syrup is boiling. Cook until syrup reaches soft ball stage (approximately 234 to 240 degrees). Test about ½ teaspoon of syrup in ice water.

Syrup should easily form a ball in ice water but flatten when held in your hand. Remove from heat; stir in peanut butter. Pour over popcorn mixture, stirring until evenly coated. Shape into 2-inch balls; place on waxed paper to cool completely. Store in an airtight container.

Yield: about 2 dozen popcorn balls

POPCORN BALL WREATH

You will need an approx. 18″ dia. artificial wreath; clear cellophane; red, white, and green ¼″w curling ribbon; approx. 2½ yds of 2⅝″w velvet ribbon; scissors; and florist wire.

1. Cut 9″ squares of cellophane. Wrap popcorn balls in cellophane, twisting ends of cellophane to secure.

2. Cut curling ribbon into 1 yd lengths. Use 1 or 2 lengths of ribbon to tie 1 end of each popcorn ball to wreath. Curl ribbon ends.

3. Form a double-loop bow from velvet ribbon; wrap wire around center of bow to secure. Cut three 1½ yd lengths of curling ribbon. Place lengths together. Knot lengths of curling ribbon around center of bow, leaving 18″ and 30″ streamers. Wire bow to top of wreath. Thread 30″ streamers through scissors handle; knot to secure. Curl ribbon ends.

DELECTABLE DELIGHT

This Nectarine Bread Pudding, a shining variation of the traditional dessert, will delight family and friends. Sliced nectarines, chopped walnuts, and whole wheat bread give an extra special flavor to the treat. A pleasing combination of spices — cinnamon, ginger, cloves, and nutmeg — further enhances the taste of the delectable dessert. A cake box decorated with fancy paper and shiny metallic ribbon makes an attractive carrier for your gift.

NECTARINE BREAD PUDDING

PUDDING

- 10 slices dry, firm whole wheat bread, cut into small pieces (about 6 cups)
- 3 cups milk
- ¾ cup firmly packed brown sugar
- ⅓ cup butter or margarine, softened
- 3 eggs
- 1 teaspoon ground cinnamon
- ¼ teaspoon ground ginger
- ¼ teaspoon ground cloves
- ¼ teaspoon ground nutmeg
- 2 cups sliced nectarines
- ½ cup chopped walnuts

TOPPING

- ½ cup granulated sugar
- ½ cup chopped walnuts
- 1 teaspoon ground cinnamon

Preheat oven to 350 degrees. For pudding, combine bread and milk in a large bowl; set aside. In another large bowl, combine next 7 ingredients; beat until smooth. Add bread mixture and mix well. Fold in nectarines and walnuts. Pour batter into a greased 9 x 13-inch pan. For topping, combine all ingredients in a medium bowl. Sprinkle evenly over. Bake 40 to 45 minutes or until a toothpick inserted in center comes out clean. Cool completely on a wire rack. Store in an airtight container in refrigerator.

Give with instructions for serving.

Bread pudding may be served warm or at room temperature. To reheat, preheat oven to 350 degrees. Bake uncovered 5 to 8 minutes or until heated through. Serve with whipped cream.

Yield: about 10 servings

For box, follow Gift Box 2 instructions, page 123. We used a 10″ x 14″ x 4″ cake box and decorated it with 1¼″ wide and ¼″ wide metallic ribbon.

FOR A CHOCOLATE LOVER

*W*ith a festive paper wreath atop its chocolate-brown lid, this clever gift box presents a preview of the wonderful treats inside. Created for a friend who loves chocolate, the squares of Chocolate-Amaretto Candy are each adorned with a tiny icing wreath. Who could resist the creamy combination of chocolate and almond flavors in these appealing candies!

CHOCOLATE-AMARETTO CANDY

1½ cups (about 10 ounces) chocolate confectioners coating (used for candy making)

¼ teaspoon amaretto-flavored oil (used for candy making)

Green decorating icing

In a small saucepan, melt chocolate over low heat. Stir in amaretto oil. Pour into ungreased candy molds. Allow to harden; remove candy from molds. Using a pastry bag fitted with a wreath tip, pipe icing onto each candy. Store in an airtight container.

Yield: about 3 dozen candies

WREATH BOX

You will need a box with lid (we used a 5¾" x 5¾" x 3" box), brown fabric, craft batting, red spray paint, tracing paper, green paper, scrap of wrapping paper, black felt-tip calligraphy pen with fine point, craft glue, and 12" of ⅞"w red satin ribbon.

1. Use lid as a pattern and cut 1 piece from batting; glue batting to top of lid. To cover lid, use craft glue and fabric and follow Steps 1 - 3 of Gift Box 1 instructions, page 123.

2. For leaves, trace leaf patterns onto tracing paper; cut out. Use patterns and cut desired number of leaves from green paper. Fold each leaf in half along fold line as indicated by dotted line on pattern.

3. Tie ribbon into a bow and trim ends.

4. For wreath, arrange leaves and bow on lid. Glue ½ of each leaf to lid to secure; glue bow to lid. Set lid aside.

5. Apply 2 coats of spray paint to box, allowing to dry between coats.

6. For label, use pen to write "To My Chocolate-Loving Friend" on green paper. Trim label to desired size. Cut a piece of wrapping paper ¼" larger on all sides than label. Glue label to wrapping paper; glue label to front of box.

HELPFUL HOLIDAY MEAL

*W*hen the holidays
*roll around, lend a helping
hand to a busy friend with
a ready-made meal! Given
early, this Spaghetti Pie can
be kept in the freezer until
it's needed after a long day
of shopping. The table runner
makes a festive companion
for the casserole.*

SPAGHETTI PIE

    6 cups water
    4 tablespoons olive oil, divided
    1 tablespoon salt
    1 pound uncooked thin spaghetti
    2 medium onions, chopped
    1 green pepper, seeded and chopped
    3 eggs, beaten
    1 container (15 ounces) ricotta
         cheese
    ¾ cup grated Parmesan cheese
    1 teaspoon dried oregano
    1 teaspoon dried basil
    ½ teaspoon crushed red pepper
         flakes
    1 cup (4 ounces) grated Cheddar
         cheese
    1 pound mild pork sausage,
         cooked, crumbled, and
         drained well

In a large stockpot, bring water,
2 tablespoons oil, and salt to a boil over
high heat. Stir in spaghetti and cook
10 to 12 minutes or until tender. Drain
and rinse with cold water; set aside.

Preheat oven to 350 degrees. In a
large skillet, heat remaining oil over
medium heat. Sauté onions and pepper
until soft; transfer to a large bowl. Add
next 6 ingredients; beat until well
blended using medium speed of an
electric mixer. Add spaghetti; toss until
well coated. Spoon ½ of spaghetti
mixture into bottoms of 2 greased 7-inch
springform pans. Spread cheese and
sausage evenly over spaghetti. Top with
remaining ½ of spaghetti mixture. Bake
30 to 35 minutes or until center of pie is
set. Cool in pans 15 minutes; remove
sides of pans. Store in an airtight
container in refrigerator. Give with
instructions to reheat.

To reheat, preheat oven to
350 degrees. Transfer pie to an
ungreased baking sheet. Cover loosely
with aluminum foil. Bake 10 to
12 minutes or until heated through.

Yield: 2 pies

TABLE RUNNER

You will need one 14″ x 36″ purchased
table runner, six 5″ long green silk fern
leaves with stems removed, six 1½″
fabric squares, six ⅝″w gold star studs,
red glitter and green dimensional fabric
paint in squeeze bottles, paper-backed
fusible web, and aluminum foil.

1. Wash, dry, and press table runner.
2. Press leaves with a warm dry iron.
Place a piece of foil on ironing board.
Place leaves and fabric squares wrong
side up on foil. Fuse web to wrong side
of leaves and squares. Remove paper
backing; remove leaves and squares
from foil and trim excess web from edges.
3. Spacing evenly, place 3 squares at
1 end of runner. Place 3 leaves on
runner with wide ends of leaves covering
top edges of squares. Fuse in place.
Repeat for remaining end of runner.
4. Apply red paint along edges of fabric
squares; allow to dry. Apply green paint
along edges of leaves; allow to dry.
Attach 1 stud to top of each tree.

27

COTTAGE CONFECTIONS

*T*hese lavishly
decorated "gingerbread"
houses look good enough to
eat — and they are! Easily
created with decorating icing
and purchased graham
crackers, the edible cottages
feature ornate trims of cake
decorations, candies, gum,
and other tasty treats. You'll
have fun making one of these
sweet little homes (or a whole
village!) for a friend.

"GINGERBREAD" HOUSES

For each house, you will need graham
crackers, purchased white decorating
icing, and items to decorate house (we
used hard candies, purchased cake
decorations, bubble gum, licorice, jelly
beans, candy-coated chocolate pieces,
chocolate bar pieces, mints,
butterscotch chips, stick gum, and
candy corn).

1. (*Note:* Use scissors to cut crackers.
Use icing to "glue" cracker pieces
together.) For front wall of house, refer
to Fig. 1 and cut corners from 1 cracker
half. Repeat for back wall.

Fig. 1

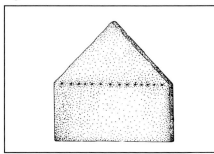

2. Refer to Fig. 2 to glue front and back
walls to 1 cracker half (base). Use props
to hold walls upright until side walls are
added.

Fig. 2

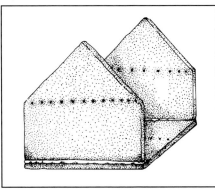

3. For side walls, glue 2 cracker
quarters to base and front and back
walls (Fig. 3). Allow icing to harden
slightly.

Fig. 3

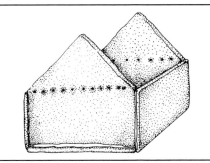

4. For roof, apply icing to top edges of
walls. Refer to Fig. 4 to place 2 cracker
halves on top of house. Apply icing
along peak of roof (Fig. 4). Allow icing
to harden for several hours or overnight
before decorating house.

Fig. 4

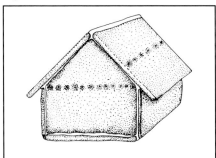

5. Use icing to attach candies and
decorative items to house for doors,
windows, shutters, chimneys, fences,
shrubbery, and roof. Allow icing to
harden.

6. Store house in an airtight container
until ready to present.

AN ELEGANT OFFERING

*O*ur Almond Cream Liqueur provides a perfect ending to a wonderful meal. Quick and easy to make, this after-dinner beverage is an elegant gift for the holidays. Present it with our fancy cordial coaster — a decoupage terra-cotta plant saucer! A gold bag with matching paper and ribbon adds a pretty touch for delivery.

ALMOND CREAM LIQUEUR

  1 can (14 ounces) sweetened
      condensed milk
1½ cups whipping cream
  1 cup almond-flavored liqueur
⅔ cup vodka
  1 teaspoon vanilla extract
  2 tablespoons almond extract

Pour all ingredients into a blender and blend until smooth. Store in an airtight container in refrigerator. Shake well before serving. Serve chilled.

Yield: about 5 cups liqueur

CORDIAL COASTER

You will need a 5¾" dia. terra-cotta plant saucer, printed tissue paper, glossy Mod Podge® sealer, foam brush, 18½" of ⅜"w satin ribbon, 23½" of ⅛"w flat gold braid, one ⅝" dia. gold button with shank removed, hot glue gun, glue sticks, and a 4" dia. circle of ⅛" thick cork.

1. (*Note:* Use sealer for gluing unless otherwise indicated; allow to dry after

each glue step.) Cut a 1" x 18½" strip, a 1½" x 18" strip, and a 9" square from tissue.

2. Apply sealer to inside of saucer and top of rim. Beginning at center, press tissue square into bottom and up sides of saucer, flattening wrinkles to form a smooth surface. Trim tissue ¼" above rim; press tissue onto rim.

3. With 1 long edge even with top edge of rim, glue 1"w tissue strip around rim, flattening wrinkles to form a smooth surface.

4. With 1 long edge under rim, glue

1½"w tissue strip to side of saucer, flattening wrinkles to form a smooth surface. Glue remaining long edge to bottom of saucer.

5. Apply 2 coats of sealer to coaster, allowing to dry between coats.

6. Glue ribbon around rim. Cut an 18½" length from braid. Glue braid over ribbon.

7. Form a loop with remaining braid; hot glue loop to rim. Hot glue button over loop. Hot glue cork to bottom of saucer.

STAIRWAY OF STARS

*T*ied with shimmering ribbon, this stairway of stars will brighten someone's holidays! The crispy chocolate Star Cookies are enhanced with ground almonds for a pleasing flavor combination. Presented with the cookies, a handwritten gift tag adorned with gold foil stars expresses a shining Christmas wish.

STAR COOKIES

- ½ cup butter or margarine, softened
- 1 cup firmly packed brown sugar
- 1 egg
- ½ teaspoon vanilla extract
- 3 ounces unsweetened chocolate, melted
- 1 cup semisweet chocolate chips, melted
- ½ cup finely ground almonds
- 2 cups all-purpose flour
- ½ teaspoon baking powder
- ¼ teaspoon baking soda
- ¼ teaspoon salt
- 3 tablespoons evaporated milk

Preheat oven to 400 degrees. In a large bowl, cream butter and sugar until fluffy. Add egg and beat until smooth. Add vanilla and chocolates, beating until smooth. Stir in nuts. In another large bowl, sift together next 4 ingredients. Stir dry ingredients alternately with milk into creamed mixture, mixing until a soft dough forms.

On a lightly floured surface, use a floured rolling pin to roll out dough to ¼-inch thickness. For patterns, follow Transferring Patterns, page 122, to cut out each size pattern. Place each pattern on dough and use a sharp knife to cut out 8 of each size cookie. Transfer cookies to a greased baking sheet. Bake 10 to 12 minutes. Cool completely on a wire rack. Starting with largest size cookie on bottom, stack 2 of each size cookie together. Tie each stack of cookies together with ribbon.

Yield: 4 stacks of 12 cookies

CHRISTMAS CHEESE CRACKERS

These Christmas Cheese Crackers are perfect for holiday giving! They're lightly spiced with cayenne pepper and a dash of steak sauce. To present the tree-shaped treats, decorate a Shaker box with appliquéd evergreens. We chose a gold background fabric to coordinate with the cheesy crackers.

CHRISTMAS CHEESE CRACKERS

- 1 cup butter or margarine, softened
- 1 cup (4 ounces) grated sharp Cheddar cheese
- 2 cups all-purpose flour
- 2 tablespoons chopped chives
- 1 teaspoon whole caraway seed
- 1 teaspoon steak sauce
- ¼ teaspoon ground cayenne pepper
- 1 tablespoon salt

Preheat oven to 350 degrees. In a large bowl, beat butter and cheese using lowest speed of an electric mixer until well blended. Add next 5 ingredients; mix until a soft dough forms. On a lightly floured surface, use a floured rolling pin to roll out dough to ¼-inch thickness. Use a tree-shaped cookie cutter to cut out crackers. Transfer to a greased baking sheet. Sprinkle salt over crackers. Bake 12 to 15 minutes or until crackers are light brown. Cool completely on a wire rack. Store in an airtight container.

Yield: about 3½ dozen crackers

APPLIQUÉD CRACKER BOX

You will need one 8½" dia. Shaker box, one 11" square of fabric to cover lid, one 5" x 16" piece of fabric for tree appliqués, thread to match appliqué fabric, fabric for trim on lid, tracing paper, fabric marking pencil, paper-backed fusible web, craft batting, and fabric glue.

1. Cut a piece of web slightly smaller than appliqué fabric. Follow manufacturer's instructions to fuse web to wrong side of fabric.
2. Trace tree pattern onto tracing paper; cut out. Use pattern and cut 4 trees from appliqué fabric.
3. Fold 11" fabric square in half from top to bottom and again from left to right. Press folds; unfold fabric and lay it right side up. Center 1 tree on each fold with top point of each tree ¼" from center of fabric. Follow manufacturer's instructions to fuse trees in place.
4. Use a medium width zigzag stitch with a short stitch length to stitch over raw edges of each tree appliqué.
5. Place appliquéd square right side down. Center lid on square and draw around lid with fabric marking pencil. Cut out fabric ½" outside drawn line. Clip fabric at ½" intervals to within ⅛" of drawn line.
6. Using lid as a pattern, cut 1 circle from batting.
7. Matching edges, place batting circle on top of lid. Center fabric circle right side up on batting. Alternating sides and pulling fabric taut, glue clipped edges of fabric to side of lid.
8. For trim, measure width of side of lid and add 1"; measure circumference of lid and add 2". Cut fabric the determined measurements. Press all edges of fabric strip ½" to wrong side. Glue strip to side of lid.

A Taste Of Italy

Tasty treats are always welcome gifts during the holidays, and our hearty Pesto Dip is sure to be a real crowd-pleaser. Flavored with basil, garlic, and Parmesan cheese, this Italian favorite is delicious served with crackers or fresh vegetables. A basket spruced up with holiday greenery and a cheery red and white checked bread cloth is a cute way to deliver the savory snack. Your friends will enjoy this taste of Italy!

PESTO DIP

    1 jar (0.6 ounces) dried
        crushed basil leaves
    ¼ cup olive oil
    1 teaspoon garlic powder
    ¼ teaspoon salt
    2 tablespoons plus 2 teaspoons
        grated Parmesan cheese
    ¼ cup pine nuts
    1 carton (16 ounces) sour cream

Place first 4 ingredients in a food processor fitted with a steel blade and process until smooth. Add cheese and nuts; process until smooth. Transfer to a large bowl. Add sour cream; stir until well blended. Store in an airtight container in refrigerator. Serve with crackers or fresh vegetables.

Yield: about 2 cups dip

For basket liner, cut a fabric square ¾" larger on all sides than desired finished size of liner. Press raw edges ⅜" to wrong side; press ⅜" to wrong side again. Use a ¼" seam allowance to stitch in place.

SHORTBREAD GREETINGS

*B*aked in a decorative shortbread mold, crisp wedges of Dipped Ginger Shortbread are an old-fashioned way to send Christmas greetings. To accompany the gingery shortbread, include a packet of handcrafted cards for your friend's holiday correspondence. Homey fabrics behind the star cutouts add to the charm of the hand-lettered verse.

DIPPED GINGER SHORTBREAD

- ½ cup butter, softened
- ⅓ cup firmly packed brown sugar
- 1 cup all-purpose flour
- ½ teaspoon ground ginger
- 1 cup (6 ounces) semisweet chocolate chips, melted

Preheat oven to 300 degrees. In a large bowl, cream butter and sugar until fluffy. In a medium bowl, sift together flour and ginger. Stir dry ingredients into creamed mixture; knead until a soft dough forms. Press dough into bottom of a greased 8-inch round shortbread mold or a 9-inch round cake pan. Prick shortbread with a fork. Bake 30 to 35 minutes or until light brown. Cool in pan 10 minutes; turn onto a cutting board. Cut into wedges while shortbread is warm. Cool completely.

Dip wide end of each piece of shortbread in chocolate. Transfer to a wire rack with waxed paper underneath to cool completely. Store in an airtight container.

Yield: about 8 pieces shortbread

STAR CARDS

For each card, you will need 2 sheets of 6¼" x 9" stationery paper, matching envelope, tracing paper, black felt-tip calligraphy pen with fine point, craft knife, cutting mat or a thick layer of newspapers, fabric scraps, craft glue, and coordinating thread.

1. For card front, match short edges and fold 1 sheet of paper in half; unfold paper and lay flat.
2. Trace star patterns onto tracing paper; cut out. Place patterns on left half of paper and draw around stars. Use pen to write ''Love was born at Christmas'' and ''Stars and angels gave the sign'' around stars. Use craft knife to cut out stars.
3. Turn paper over. Cut fabric scraps to cover star openings; glue scraps over openings.

4. With decorated side right side up, refold paper. Insert 1 end of remaining sheet of paper between halves of decorated sheet as shown in Fig. 1. Stitching approximately ¼" from edges of card front, machine stitch through all 3 layers of paper. Knot thread ends on inside of card; trim ends. Fold card in half.

Fig. 1

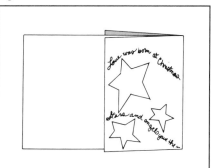

A Spirited Noel

Lighter in texture than traditional fruitcake, ginger-spiced Noel Cakes are laden with dried apricots and cherries, candied pineapple, and pecans. Buttery Orange Sauce, flavored with orange liqueur, makes a delectable topping for the moist cake. For an elegant presentation, place one of the fruitcakes and a bottle of the spirited sauce on a brass tray lined with a festive cloth.

NOEL CAKES WITH ORANGE SAUCE

CAKE

- ⅔ cup chopped dried apricots
- 1 container (4 ounces) candied pineapple
- ½ cup all-purpose flour, divided
- 1 cup dried cherries, pitted
- 1 cup orange-flavored liqueur
- 6 tablespoons butter or margarine, softened
- ¼ cup firmly packed brown sugar
- 2 tablespoons finely chopped crystallized ginger
- ½ teaspoon ground cinnamon
- ¼ teaspoon ground nutmeg
- ⅛ teaspoon ground cloves
- 2 eggs
- 1 cup chopped pecans

ORANGE SAUCE

- 1 cup butter or margarine
- 1 cup firmly packed brown sugar
- 1 cup orange-flavored liqueur

In a food processor fitted with a steel blade, process apricots, pineapple, and 2 teaspoons flour until coarsely chopped. Combine apricot mixture, cherries, and liqueur in a medium saucepan. Cook over medium heat until mixture begins to boil; remove from heat. Drain fruit, reserving liquid for sauce.

Preheat oven to 350 degrees. Place remaining flour and next 6 ingredients in a food processor fitted with a steel blade; process until a soft dough forms. Add eggs; process until smooth. Transfer mixture to a large bowl. Stir in nuts and drained fruit. Pour batter evenly into 2 greased 3½" x 5-inch loaf pans. Bake 20 to 25 minutes or until a toothpick inserted in center comes out clean. Cool 10 minutes in pans; turn onto a wire rack to cool completely. Store in an airtight container.

For sauce, combine butter and sugar in a medium saucepan over medium heat. Bring to a boil, stirring constantly until sugar is dissolved. Remove from heat; whisk in reserved liquid and liqueur. Store in an airtight container in refrigerator. Give with instructions to serve.

Serve sauce warm with cake. To reheat, transfer sauce to a medium saucepan. Cook over medium heat 2 to 3 minutes, stirring constantly until heated through.

Yield: 2 cakes

A GOURMET GIFT

*F*or a Yuletide gift with European flavor, present a bottle of Pear Wine in a ribbon-tied basket. The mellow beverage is easy to make by adding fresh fruit and sugar to white wine, and it's wonderful served with fresh bread sticks or cheese. A simple wax seal gives the bottle a gourmet look.

PEAR WINE

  4 ripe Bartlett pears
  1 bottle (720 ml) dry white wine
  ¼ cup granulated sugar

Wash and core pears; cut into small cubes. Combine pears and remaining ingredients in a large bowl; stir until sugar dissolves. Pour into bottle and chill 3 days to allow flavors to blend. Store in an airtight container in refrigerator.

Yield: about 3 cups wine

For wax seal on top of bottle, follow Sealing Bottle With Wax instructions, page 122.

EASY CHRISTMAS COOKIES

*W*ith our simple decorating tips, it's easy to transform store-bought cookies into fun treats to share during Christmastime. Purchased icing, cinnamon candies, and shiny dragées turn plain cookies into holly-trimmed wreaths and poinsettia-adorned gift boxes. Cookies dipped in almond bark and topped with almond "flames" stand upright on chocolate sandwich cookies to make our unique Candle Cookies. These cute creations are sure to be delightful conversation pieces!

CANDLE COOKIES

Vanilla-flavored almond bark
Pepperidge Farms® Pirouette
   cookies
Purchased green decorating icing
Chocolate sandwich cookies
Whole almonds

Melt almond bark in a small saucepan according to package directions. Using tongs, dip each Pirouette cookie in almond bark, coating completely. Place on a wire rack with waxed paper underneath to cool completely.

Using a large star tip, pipe icing in a small circle on 1 side of each sandwich cookie. Place 1 end of a dipped cookie in icing. Using a small amount of icing,
secure 1 almond in remaining end of dipped cookie. Allow icing to harden. Store in an airtight container.

WREATH COOKIES

Wreath-shaped cookies
Purchased green decorating icing
Red cinnamon candies

Using a small leaf tip, pipe icing onto each cookie to resemble leaves. Place candies in center of leaves. Allow icing to harden. Store in an airtight container.

GIFT BOX COOKIES

Square shortbread cookies
Purchased red and green decorating
   icing
Gold dragées

Using a small leaf tip, pipe green icing onto each cookie to resemble ribbon. Using a small round tip, pipe red icing onto each cookie to resemble a poinsettia. Place a dragée in center of each flower. Allow icing to harden. Store in an airtight container.

COZY MINI LOAVES

Sharing your holiday baking has never been easier! Our recipe for Swiss Cheese Bread makes seven mellow mini loaves, and the festive fabric cozy keeps each loaf warm for delivery fresh from the oven.

SWISS CHEESE BREAD

- 4 cups all-purpose flour
- 2 tablespoons granulated sugar
- 1 tablespoon baking powder
- 1½ teaspoons salt
- ½ cup butter or margarine, chilled and cut into pieces
- 4 cups (16 ounces) grated Swiss cheese
- 1 tablespoon dried dill weed
- 2 cups milk
- 2 eggs

Preheat oven to 400 degrees. In a large bowl, combine first 4 ingredients. Using a pastry blender or 2 knives, cut butter into flour mixture until mixture resembles coarse meal. Stir in cheese and dill. In a medium bowl, whisk together milk and eggs. Add milk mixture to flour mixture; stir just until moistened. Pour batter evenly into 7 greased 3 x 5½-inch loaf pans. Bake 20 to 25 minutes or until a toothpick inserted in center comes out clean. Cool 10 minutes in pan; turn onto a wire rack to cool completely. Store in an airtight container. Give with instructions for reheating.

To reheat, preheat oven to 300 degrees. Bake uncovered 3 to 5 minutes or until heated through.

Yield: 7 mini loaves bread

MINI LOAF COZY

You will need desired fabric, craft batting, 1 yd of ⅛"w grosgrain ribbon, and thread to match fabric and ribbon.

1. Measure outside of loaf pan from side rim to side rim; measure outside of pan from end rim to end rim. Add 1" to each measurement; cut 2 pieces of fabric and 1 piece of batting the determined measurements.
2. Place fabric pieces right sides together on top of batting piece. Leaving an opening for turning, use a ½" seam allowance and stitch all layers together. Turn right side out and press; sew final closure by hand.
3. For sides of cozy, measure height of loaf pan and subtract ¼". Measuring from 1 corner of cozy, mark the determined measurement on short edge with a pin; mark the determined measurement on long edge with a pin. Referring to Fig. 1, match pins and fold cozy diagonally; sew across point (Fig. 1). Repeat for each corner.

Fig. 1

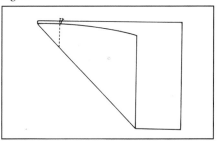

4. Cut four 9" lengths from ribbon. Tie each length into a bow; trim ends. Tack 1 bow to each corner of cozy.

NUT-CRACKER SWEETS

*C*ashews and oyster crackers are combined with semisweet chocolate and cinnamon to create these rich Nut-Cracker Sweets. Cleverly presented in our ''nutcracker'' canister, the candy is sure to be as popular as the traditional Christmas character. What a fun holiday gift!

NUT-CRACKER SWEETS

1 package (12 ounces) semisweet
  chocolate chips
3 tablespoons ground cinnamon
1 cup unsalted cashews
1 cup oyster crackers

Melt chocolate in a medium saucepan
over low heat. Stir in cinnamon. Fold in
cashews and crackers. Drop by heaping
teaspoonfuls onto waxed paper. Cool
completely. Store in airtight container.

Yield: about 2½ dozen candies

NUTCRACKER CANISTER

You will need a 7"h x 4" dia. cardboard
canister with resealable lid (we used an
18 oz. oatmeal package); blue and
metallic gold spray paint; a 3¼" dia.
plastic foam ball; paring knife; instant
papier mâché (we used Celluclay®
Instant Papier Mâché); gesso; white,
peach, pink, red, blue, and black acrylic
paint; foam brushes; paintbrushes; a
4" square of white artificial fur; a
½" dia. red bead for nose; 4" of ⅛"w
gold braid; four ⅝" dia. gold metal
buttons; 14" of ⅝"w black satin
ribbon; lightweight cardboard; a
2¼" x 11½" strip of shiny black
wrapping paper; a ½" dia. VELCRO®
brand fastener; hot glue gun; and glue
sticks.

1. For head shape, use knife to cut ¼"
from 1 side of plastic foam ball, forming
a flat surface (bottom).
2. Follow Papier Mâché instructions,
page 122, to apply papier mâché over
head shape.
3. Apply 1 coat of gesso and 1 coat of
peach paint to head, allowing to dry
between coats.
4. Use a pencil to lightly sketch face
pattern onto head.

5. Mix 1 part pink paint to 1 part water.
Use diluted paint to paint cheeks. Allow
to dry.
6. Referring to photo for colors and
allowing to dry after each color, paint
face. Glue bead to face for nose.
7. Cut two 1½" x 1¾" strips from fur
for hair and one ¾" x 2" strip for
beard. Fold long edges of each hair strip
¼" to wrong side; glue in place. With
wrong side facing head, glue 1 hair strip
to each side of head. With right side of
beard strip facing bottom of head, center
and glue 1 end of strip below mouth.
8. For hat, cut a 2¼" x 11½" strip
from cardboard. For belt buckle, cut a
1" x 1½" piece from cardboard. Cut a
½" x 1" piece from center of buckle
piece and discard.
9. Spray paint cardboard pieces and
canister lid gold. Spray paint canister
blue. Allow to dry.

10. For hat decoration, cut 1½" long
V-shaped notches along 1 long edge of
wrapping paper. Matching long straight
edge of decoration to 1 long edge of hat
strip, glue decoration to hat strip.
11. Overlapping ends 1", glue ends of
hat strip together. Glue hat to head.
12. For belt, wrap ribbon around canister
approximately 2¼" from bottom; glue
to secure. Glue buckle over ribbon at
center front.
13. Cut braid in half. With 1 length 1"
above belt and remaining length 2¼"
above belt, glue braid to center front of
canister. Glue 1 button over each end of
braid.
14. Glue 1 side of VELCRO® fastener to
center top of lid. Glue remaining side to
center bottom of head.
15. Place a plastic bag of candy in
canister, place lid on canister, and
attach head to lid.

CHEERY CHERRY TEA

CHERRY TEA MIX

1 package (0.14 ounces)
   unsweetened cherry-flavored
   soft drink mix
$1\frac{1}{4}$ cups sugar-free instant tea mix
   (artificially sweetened)

Combine ingredients in a small bowl; stir until well blended. Store in an airtight container. Give with instructions for serving.

To serve, stir 2 teaspoons tea mix into 8 ounces hot or cold water.

Yield: $1\frac{1}{4}$ cups tea mix

SANTA MUG

You will need a Crafter's Pride Stitch-A-Mug with Vinyl-Weave® (14 ct) insert and embroidery floss (see color key).

1. Follow manufacturer's instructions to remove insert from mug.
2. With bottom edge of design 8 fabric squares from 1 long edge of insert and right edge of design 20 fabric squares from 1 short edge of insert, work design using 2 strands of floss for Cross Stitch and 1 for Backstitch.
3. With short edges aligned with handle, place insert in mug. Reassemble mug. Hand wash mug to protect stitchery.

*E*ven Santa will find it easy to watch his waistline during the holidays with this sugar-free Cherry Tea Mix! The rich, ruby-hued beverage has a deliciously fruity flavor that will appeal to non-dieters, too. Presented along with the mix and its serving instructions, a cross-stitched mug features the jolly Christmas gentleman with his pack of toys.

SANTA (35w x 35h)

X	DMC	¼X	B'ST	JPC	COLOR
	blanc			1001	white
C	309			3284	lt red
	310	◢	◿	8403	black
	319	◢		6246	dk green
S	320			6017	green
X	435			5371	tan
-	437	◩	◿	5942	lt tan
⊙	451	◩	◿		grey
+	453	◻			lt grey

X	DMC	¼X	B'ST	JPC	COLOR
✳	498			3410	red
	640	◢		5393	beige grey
◇	729			5363	gold
□	754	◻		2331	peach
★	814	◢		3044	dk red
A	962	◩		3151	pink
8	3328			3071	salmon
2	3347	◢		6266	lt green
•	310		black French Knot		

SANTA (35w x 35h)			
Aida 11	3¼"	x	3¼"
Aida 14	2½"	x	2½"
Aida 18	2"	x	2"
Hardanger 22	1⅝"	x	1⅝"

CUPCAKE BASKET

*L*ight, crisp meringue filled with chocolate chips and pecans is nestled atop a chocolate crust to create these Chocolate Meringue Cupcakes. To cradle the airy delights, we crafted a basket from aluminum flashing and added a bow of wired ribbon. A simple spray painting technique provides the look of antique pewter.

CHOCOLATE MERINGUE CUPCAKES

CRUST

- 16 2-inch diameter chocolate wafer cookies, finely ground
- 3 tablespoons butter or margarine, melted
- 1 teaspoon ground cinnamon

FILLING

- 3 egg whites
- ⅔ cup granulated sugar
- ½ teaspoon ground cinnamon
- ½ cup semisweet chocolate chips
- ½ cup chopped pecans

For crust, combine all ingredients in a medium bowl; stir until well blended. Press about 2 teaspoons mixture into bottom of each paper-lined muffin tin.

Preheat oven to 325 degrees. For filling, beat egg whites in a large bowl until foamy. Add sugar and cinnamon; beat until stiff. Fold in remaining ingredients. Spoon about 2 tablespoons filling into each muffin tin. Bake 30 to 35 minutes or until light brown and set in center. Cool completely in pan. Store in an airtight container.

Yield: about 1½ dozen cupcakes

''PEWTER'' BASKET

You will need aluminum flashing (available at hardware stores), utility scissors, 1 yd of 1″w wired plastic ribbon, ruler, hammer, slip-joint pliers, sandpaper, hot glue gun, glue sticks, flat grey and flat black spray paint, and a fabric square to line basket.

1. (*Note:* Cut edges of flashing may be sharp.) Cut a 6¼″ x 25″ piece for basket and a 1½″ x 18″ strip for handle from flashing.
2. Refer to Diagram and use a pencil to mark cutting lines (dotted lines) and fold lines (grey lines) on 1 side (wrong side) of basket piece. Repeat for handle strip.
3. For top edge of basket, place ruler against fold line A and fold flashing to wrong side over ruler. Remove ruler and use hammer to tightly crease flashing at fold. Repeat to fold long edges of handle strip to wrong side along fold lines.
4. Use pliers to crimp top edge of basket.
5. Cut basket piece along cutting lines. Place ruler against fold line B and fold bottom flaps to wrong side, forming a 90 degree angle. Place ruler against each remaining fold line and bend flashing to form a box, allowing bottom flaps to overlap.
6. (*Note:* Before gluing, lightly sand areas of flashing to be glued.) Glue right side of flap to inside of basket. Glue bottom flaps together. Bend handle to wrong side, forming a curve. Glue handle to inside of basket at each end.
7. Spray paint both sides of ribbon grey; allow to dry. Tie ribbon into a bow; trim and arrange streamers as desired.
8. Lightly spray basket with grey paint; allow to dry. Holding paint can about 12″ away, lightly spray basket and bow with black paint; allow to dry.
9. Glue bow to basket handle. Line basket with fabric square.

DIAGRAM

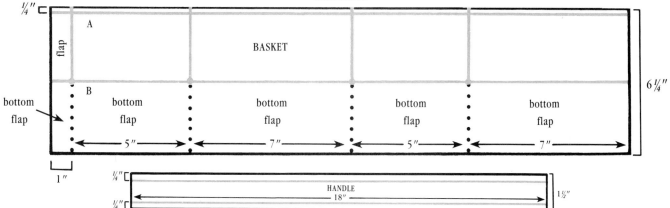

SCOTTISH GREETINGS

This year, you can deliver your season's greetings in Scottish style. Cut in a wreath shape, crispy Butterscotch Cookies are gaily decorated with red icing bows and green candy pieces. The cookies look right at home in a Shaker box covered with Christmasy tartan plaid fabric. What a cute way to send a holiday "hello"!

BUTTERSCOTCH COOKIES

- ½ cup butter or margarine, softened
- ⅓ cup granulated sugar
- ⅓ cup firmly packed brown sugar
- 1 egg
- 1 teaspoon vanilla extract
- 1 cup butterscotch chips, melted
- 2⅓ cups all-purpose flour
- ¾ teaspoon baking soda
  Purchased red decorating icing
  Green candy-coated chocolate pieces

Preheat oven to 375 degrees. In a large bowl, cream butter and sugars until fluffy. Add egg and vanilla, mixing until smooth. Stir in melted butterscotch chips. In another large bowl, sift together flour and baking soda. Stir dry ingredients into creamed mixture. On a lightly floured surface, use a floured rolling pin to roll out dough to ¼-inch thickness. Use a doughnut cutter to cut out dough. Transfer cookies to a greased baking sheet. Bake 8 to 10 minutes or until brown. Cool completely on a wire rack. Use decorating icing and candy-coated pieces to decorate cookies.

Yield: about 2½ dozen 3-inch cookies

TARTAN PLAID BOX

You will need a round Shaker box, plaid fabric, grosgrain ribbon the width of side of lid, craft glue, desired color acrylic paint, and foam brush.

1. Paint inside of box and lid; allow to dry.
2. To cover lid, cut a fabric circle ½" larger than top of lid. Center lid on wrong side of circle. At ½" intervals, make cuts into edge of fabric to ⅛" from lid. Glue cut edges of fabric to side of lid. Glue ribbon to side of lid, covering raw edges of fabric. Allow to dry.
3. To cover box, measure circumference of box and add ½"; measure height of box. Cut fabric the determined measurements. Overlapping short edges, glue fabric to side of box. Allow to dry.

BRAIDED BREAKFAST RING

What hostess wouldn't love this pretty — and edible — centerpiece for her holiday breakfast table! With a sweet orange glaze and a brown-sugary filling of cinnamon, walnuts, and orange peel, our delectable Braided Orange Bread is sure to be appreciated. Silk greenery and a festive candle complete the arrangement.

BRAIDED ORANGE BREAD

BREAD

- 4½ cups all-purpose flour
- 2 packages quick-rising dry yeast
- 1½ teaspoons salt
- 6 tablespoons butter or margarine
- ½ cup milk
- ½ cup water
- 1 egg
- 1 teaspoon vanilla extract

FILLING

- 1 cup butter or margarine
- 2 cups firmly packed brown sugar
- 2 cups finely chopped walnuts
- 2 tablespoons ground cinnamon
- 1 tablespoon grated dried orange peel

GLAZE

- 2 tablespoons frozen orange juice concentrate, thawed
- 2 tablespoons granulated sugar

For bread, combine first 3 ingredients in a large bowl, mixing well. In a medium saucepan, melt butter over medium heat; stir in milk and water. Heat mixture to approximately 130 degrees. Remove from heat. Whisk egg and vanilla into milk mixture. Stir milk mixture into dry ingredients; knead until a soft dough forms. Turn dough onto a lightly floured surface and knead about 5 minutes or until dough becomes elastic. Divide dough in half, cover, and let rest at room temperature.

For filling, combine all ingredients in a medium saucepan. Bring to a boil over medium heat, stirring constantly until sugar dissolves (about 3 minutes). Remove from heat; set aside.

For glaze, combine orange juice and sugar in a small bowl. Stir until sugar dissolves; set aside.

On a lightly floured surface, use a floured rolling pin to roll out each half of dough to a 6 x 20-inch rectangle. Spread half of filling evenly over each rectangle. Cut each rectangle into three 2-inch wide strips. With filling sides together, fold strips in half lengthwise. Braid 3 strips of dough together; join ends to form a circle. Repeat for remaining strips of dough. Transfer to a greased baking sheet. Cover and set in a warm place (80 to 85 degrees). Let rise 30 minutes or until doubled in size.

Preheat oven to 375 degrees. Bake 8 to 9 minutes; brush generously with glaze. Bake 4 to 5 minutes longer or until golden brown. Remove from oven; brush with remaining glaze. Cool completely on a wire rack. Store in an airtight container. Give with instructions to serve.

Bread may be served at room temperature or warm. To reheat, preheat oven to 350 degrees. Bake uncovered on an ungreased baking sheet 3 to 5 minutes or until heated through.

Yield: 2 bread rings

MERRY "CHRIS MOUSE"

Your friends will know Christmas is near when this merry mouse shows up at their house. Imagine their surprise when they discover that the delightful little fellow is actually a bag filled with savory Cheese Wafers! The crackers get their pleasing flavor from a combination of cheeses and a variety of spices. After the last cracker crumbs are gone, the cheerful mouse can be stuffed with fiberfill to make a charming Christmas decoration.

CHEESE WAFERS

- ¼ cup butter or margarine, softened
- 1 package (3 ounces) cream cheese, softened
- 2 cups (8 ounces) grated sharp Cheddar cheese
- 1¼ cups all-purpose flour
- ¼ teaspoon ground oregano
- ¼ teaspoon crushed basil leaves
- ¼ teaspoon ground sage
- ¼ teaspoon ground thyme
- ¼ teaspoon ground cayenne pepper
- 2 tablespoons dry white wine

In a large bowl, beat butter and cream cheese until fluffy. Stir in Cheddar cheese. In another large bowl, sift together next 6 ingredients. Add dry ingredients and wine alternately to cheese mixture. Knead until a stiff dough forms. Shape into 1½-inch diameter log shape and cover with plastic wrap. Chill 1 hour or until firm.

Preheat oven to 375 degrees. Cut dough into ⅛-inch thick slices. Transfer to a greased baking sheet. Bake 15 to 18 minutes or until edges are brown. Cool completely on a wire rack. Store in an airtight container.

Yield: about 4 dozen wafers

CHRIS MOUSE

You will need two 7″ squares of fabric for head, four 4″ x 6″ pieces of fabric for arms, four 5″ squares of fabric for feet, two 6″ x 7″ pieces of fabric for sleeves, one 9″ x 20″ piece of fabric for pajamas, thread to match fabrics, black embroidery floss, tracing paper, small crochet hook (to turn fabric), polyester fiberfill, black permanent felt-tip pen with fine point, fabric marking pencil, ½″ dia. black shank button with shank removed, three 4″ lengths of 24-gauge cloth-covered florist wire, black and

white acrylic paint, small paintbrushes, 1¼ yds of ⅛″w satin ribbon, one 2½″ x 6″ piece of cardboard, seam ripper, hot glue gun, and glue sticks.

1. Use patterns and follow Transferring Patterns and Sewing Shapes, page 122, to make 1 head, 2 arms, and 2 feet from fabric pieces. Stuff shapes with fiberfill; sew final closures by hand.

2. For ears, refer to dotted lines on pattern and hand sew along base of each ear through all thicknesses.

3. Use pen to draw over eyes, mouth, and teeth. Paint teeth white; allow to dry. For whiskers, paint wire lengths black; allow to dry. Glue centers of wire lengths to back of button; glue button to face.

4. For feet, thread needle with black floss; knot 1 end. Bring needle through foot at 1 ●, over top of foot, and back through foot, coming out at same ●; pull floss tight. Repeat to make a second stitch at same ●; knot and secure floss end. Repeat for remaining ●'s.

5. For sleeves, match right sides and fold 1 sleeve piece in half lengthwise.

Using a ½″ seam allowance, sew along long edge and 1 short edge. Press remaining raw edge 1½″ to wrong side. Clip corners and turn right side out. Repeat for remaining sleeve.

6. Insert 1 arm into 1 sleeve. Cut a 13″ length from ribbon. Tie ribbon length into a bow around sleeve and arm to secure. Repeat for remaining arm.

7. For pajamas, follow Steps 2 and 4 of Fabric Bag instructions, page 123. For casing, press top edge of bag ¼″ to wrong side; press ¾″ to wrong side again. Stitch ⅝″ from top edge of bag. Use seam ripper to open casing on inside of bag at 1 seamline. Thread remaining ribbon through casing. Knot each end of ribbon.

8. Place cardboard in bottom of bag. Center head along top edge on front of bag; whipstitch head in place along top of casing. Whipstitch 1 sleeve to each side seam 1¾″ from top edge of bag. Glue feet to front of bag.

9. Place a plastic bag of cheese wafers in pajama bag. Pull ribbon ends to close top of bag.

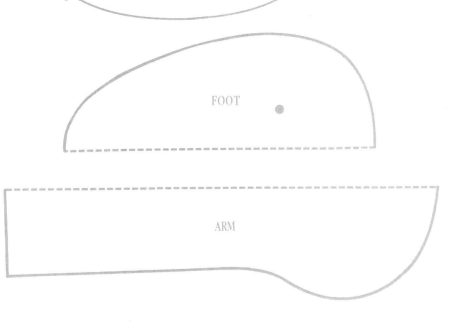

"SHRIMPLY" DELICIOUS

For a hostess gift that's "shrimply" delicious, take along this rich, spreadable Shrimp Cheese Ball. The creamy spread, seasoned with green onion, sweet basil, and rosemary, is loaded with delectable shrimp. Nestled in a little sleigh with crackers for serving, it's ready to go to any holiday gathering.

SHRIMP CHEESE BALL

1 package (8 ounces) cream cheese, softened
6 ounces (1½ cups) Havarti cheese, grated
4 green onions, chopped
2 teaspoons crushed dried basil leaves
1 teaspoon dried rosemary
1 teaspoon salt
1 package (6 ounces) frozen peeled and cooked shrimp, thawed, drained, and finely chopped
Paprika to garnish

In a large bowl, beat cream cheese until fluffy. Add next 6 ingredients; stir until well blended. Divide cheese mixture in half; form each half into a ball. Sprinkle each cheese ball with paprika. Cover and chill 8 hours or overnight to allow flavors to blend. Serve with crackers or bread. Store in an airtight container in refrigerator.

Yield: 2 cheese balls

FESTIVE FOOD BASKET

*I*nstead of buying expensive food baskets for gifts this year, why not create your own for the special families on your list! A wicker picnic hamper makes an attractive carrier for a selection of deli-style cold cuts, breads, and condiments. For a festive touch, you'll want to include our spicy Cranberry Ketchup. It's delicious on turkey sandwiches!

CRANBERRY KETCHUP

  1 can (16 ounces) jellied cranberry
        sauce
  ¾ cup granulated sugar
  ¼ cup white vinegar
  2 teaspoons ground ginger
  ¼ teaspoon ground cinnamon
  ⅛ teaspoon ground black pepper
  ⅛ teaspoon ground allspice
  1 tablespoon all-purpose flour
  2 tablespoons hot water

In a large saucepan, combine first 7 ingredients over medium heat. Bring to a boil. In a small bowl, stir flour and water together to make a paste. Add flour paste to cranberry mixture, stirring until mixture thickens. Remove from heat. Cover and chill 8 hours or overnight to allow flavors to blend. Store in an airtight container in refrigerator. Serve with meat or cream cheese and crackers.

Yield: about 2½ cups ketchup

These goodies look — and taste — like they came from a gourmet candy shop! To create the sweets, peppermint canes and chocolate sandwich cookies are dipped in candy coatings and decorated with colorful icing. Our painted tin is dressed up with red and white stripes to add joy to your gift.

CHRISTMAS DIPPED COOKIES

  6 ounces chocolate-flavored almond bark
  6 ounces vanilla-flavored almond bark
  1 package (16 ounces) chocolate sandwich cookies
      Purchased red, green, and white decorating icing

Melt chocolate and vanilla almond bark in separate small saucepans following package directions. Using tongs, dip half of cookies in chocolate almond bark. Dip remaining cookies in vanilla almond bark. Place on a wire rack to cool completely. Use decorating icing to decorate cookies. Allow icing to harden. Store in an airtight container.

Yield: 3½ dozen cookies

CHRISTMAS CANDY CANES

CANDY

  4 ounces chocolate-flavored almond bark
  4 ounces vanilla-flavored almond bark
  2 dozen small peppermint candy canes

ICING

  1 cup confectioners sugar
  1 tablespoon milk
      Red and green paste food coloring

Melt chocolate and vanilla almond bark in separate small saucepans following package directions. Using tongs, dip half of candy canes in chocolate almond bark. Dip remaining candy canes in vanilla almond bark. Place on a wire rack to cool completely.

For icing, combine sugar and milk in a small bowl, stirring until smooth. Divide icing in half. Tint 1 bowl red and 1 bowl green. Drizzle icing over candy canes. Allow icing to harden. Store in an airtight container.

Yield: 2 dozen candy canes

JOY TIN

You will need a 6½" dia. tin, green and matte white spray paint, red and white acrylic paint, small round paintbrush, matte clear acrylic spray, tracing paper, and graphite transfer paper.

1. Apply 2 coats of white spray paint to entire tin and inside of lid, allowing to dry between coats.
2. Apply 1 coat of green spray paint to top and sides of lid; allow to dry.
3. Trace ''JOY'' pattern onto tracing paper. Use transfer paper to transfer design to center of lid. Paint design, allowing to dry between colors.
4. For stripes on side of tin, use a pencil and ruler to lightly draw an even number of diagonal lines ½" apart on tin.
5. Paint alternating stripes red; allow to dry.
6. Apply 2 coats of acrylic spray to entire tin, allowing to dry between coats.

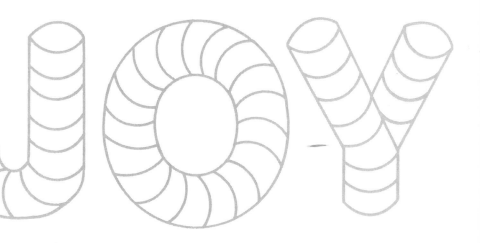

HOLIDAY BREAKFAST TRAY

This early morning treat will be a bright beginning to a special someone's day. A great topper for English muffins, our delicious Cranberry Butter is easy to make by adding whole cranberry sauce and grated orange peel to ordinary butter. A painted tray lined with wrapping paper allows you to present your gift with holiday flair.

CRANBERRY BUTTER

  2 cups butter, softened
  1 can (16 ounces) whole cranberry sauce
  1 tablespoon grated dried orange peel

In a large bowl, mix all ingredients together using lowest speed of an electric mixer. Spoon butter into molds or waxed paper-lined Shaker boxes. Cover and chill until firm. Store in refrigerator. Serve with bread or crackers.

Yield: about 3 cups butter

BREAKFAST TRAY

You will need a wooden tray, acrylic paint, wrapping paper, matte Mod Podge® sealer, and foam brushes.

1. Paint tray; allow to dry.
2. Cut a piece of wrapping paper to fit in bottom of tray. Use sealer to glue paper into tray. Allow to dry.
3. Apply 2 coats of sealer to entire tray, allowing to dry between coats.

CHRISTMAS EVE WARMER

*W*hile St. Nicholas is busily delivering gifts on Christmas Eve, a special friend can relax by a cozy fire and enjoy this warming Mocha Liqueur. A blend of cocoa, coffee, and marshmallow cream enhances the drink's rich flavor. To present your surprise, slip the bottle of liqueur into our elegant bag lined with gold lamé fabric.

MOCHA LIQUEUR

- ½ cup cocoa
- ½ cup hot brewed coffee
- 1 can (14 ounces) sweetened condensed milk
- 2 tablespoons instant coffee granules
- 1 cup marshmallow cream
- 1 cup brandy
- 1 cup coffee-flavored liqueur

In a small bowl, combine cocoa and brewed coffee, stirring until cocoa is dissolved. Combine coffee mixture and remaining ingredients in a blender or a food processor fitted with a steel blade; blend until smooth. Cover and chill overnight to allow flavors to blend. Store in an airtight container in refrigerator. Serve chilled.

Yield: about 5½ cups liqueur

BOTTLE BAG

You will need one 7" x 32" fabric piece for bag, one 7" x 32" fabric piece for lining, thread to match fabrics, ⅞ yd of ⅛" dia. twisted satin cord, and two ⅜" dia. beads.

1. Follow Steps 2 and 4 of Fabric Bag instructions, page 123, to make bag from bag fabric.
2. Leaving a 3" opening at center of 1 side of lining, repeat Step 1 for lining fabric. Do not turn lining right side out.

3. With right sides facing, insert bag into lining. Use a ¼" seam allowance and sew lining and bag together along top edge. Turn right side out through opening in side seam of lining; sew final closure by hand. Insert lining into bag and press.
4. Thread 1 bead onto each end of cord; knot and trim ends. Place bottle in bag. Tie cord into a bow around bag.

"BEARY" SWEET

A friend will be "beary" pleased to receive this Christmasy basket filled with Ginger Bears. A spoonful of strawberry preserves baked in the center of each of the spicy gingerbread cookies is a sweet surprise. The lovable bear perched on the basket handle is busy decorating for Christmas, with a garland in one hand and a stocking in the other. Even though the treats will soon be gone, the basket will be enjoyed for years to come!

GINGER BEARS

- 2 cups all-purpose flour
- ⅓ cup granulated sugar
- 1 teaspoon ground cinnamon
- 1 teaspoon ground ginger
- 1 teaspoon baking powder
- ¼ teaspoon baking soda
- ½ cup butter or margarine
- ½ cup molasses
- 2 tablespoons hot water
- ½ cup strawberry preserves
  Purchased brown decorating icing
  Red candy-coated chocolate
    pieces

In a large bowl, sift together first 6 ingredients. In a small saucepan, melt butter over low heat. Add molasses; stir until dissolved. Pour butter mixture and water into dry ingredients; knead until a soft dough forms. Cover and chill 1 hour.

Preheat oven to 375 degrees. On a lightly floured surface, use a floured rolling pin to roll out dough to ⅛-inch thickness. Follow Transferring Patterns, page 122, to cut out bear head pattern. Place pattern on dough and use a sharp knife to cut out an even number of cookies. Place ½ of cookies on greased baking sheets. Spoon about 1 teaspoon preserves in center of each cookie. Top with remaining cookies and crimp edges with a fork. Bake 10 to 12 minutes or until brown. Cool completely on a wire rack. For eyes and mouth, use a small round tip to pipe icing on each cookie. For nose, use a small amount of icing to secure a candy-coated piece on cookie. Allow icing to harden. Store in an airtight container.

Yield: about 2 dozen cookies

BEAR BASKET

You will need a basket with handle, two 5" squares of fabric for head, two 5" x 8" pieces of fabric for body, four 4" x 5" pieces of fabric for legs, two 3" x 5" pieces of fabric for stocking, fabric for basket liner, thread to match fabrics, tracing paper, fabric marking pencil, small crochet hook (to turn fabric), polyester fiberfill, brown permanent fabric marker with fine point, hot glue gun, glue sticks, two ½" dia. buttons, 6" of embroidery floss or heavy thread, and miniature greenery garland.

1. Use patterns and follow Transferring Patterns and Sewing Shapes, page 122, to make 1 head, 1 body, 2 legs, and 1 stocking from fabric pieces. Do not turn stocking right side out.
2. For bear, lightly stuff head, body, and legs with fiberfill. Sew final closures by hand. For ears and arms, refer to dotted lines on pattern and machine stitch along base of each ear and arm through all thicknesses.
3. Use marker to draw over facial features and paws.
4. Tack head to body. Sew 1 leg and 1 button to each side of body.
5. For stocking, trim top edge along pencil line; press top edge ¼" to wrong side and tack in place. Turn stocking right side out.
6. Glue bear to basket handle. Glue garland around handle; glue 1 end to 1 paw. Use floss to hang stocking ½" from remaining paw.
7. For liner, cut a fabric piece 1" larger on all sides than desired finished size. Press all edges of fabric piece ½" to wrong side; press ½" to wrong side again and stitch in place.

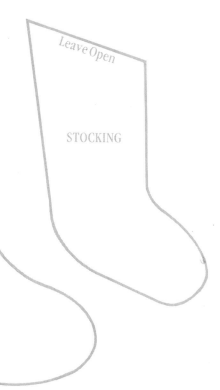

Leave Open

STOCKING

Holiday Casserole

Spicy Saffron Shrimp is sure to be warmly received when you take it to a holiday dinner party — or when you want to treat a friend to a heat-and-serve meal. A blend of saffron and other spices, along with yogurt and ground peanuts, gives the casserole its unusual flavor. A stenciled basket cradles the dish in festive style, and the matching kitchen towels can be enjoyed throughout the season.

SAFFRON SHRIMP

1 can (10½ ounces) chicken broth
½ teaspoon ground saffron
1 tablespoon olive oil
1 large onion, finely chopped
4 cloves garlic, minced
1 cup unsalted roasted peanuts
1 cup plain yogurt
2 teaspoons chopped crystallized ginger
2 teaspoons ground coriander
1 teaspoon ground cumin
1 teaspoon ground cardamom
½ teaspoon salt
¼ teaspoon ground black pepper
2 packages (6 ounces each) frozen cooked and peeled shrimp, thawed and drained
3 cups cooked white rice

In a small saucepan, heat chicken broth over medium heat until boiling; remove from heat. Stir in saffron; set aside. In a small skillet, heat oil over medium heat. Sauté onion and garlic until brown. In a blender or food processor fitted with a steel blade, process peanuts until finely ground. Add onion mixture, broth mixture, and next 7 ingredients to food processor; process until well blended. Transfer to a large bowl; stir in shrimp and rice. Pour into a 1½-quart casserole dish. Cover and refrigerate until ready to present. Give with instructions for reheating.

To reheat, preheat oven to 375 degrees. Cover and bake 20 to 25 minutes or until heated through. Store in covered container in refrigerator.

Yield: 6 to 8 servings

STENCILED TOWELS AND BASKET

For each towel, you will need a 15" x 24" piece of osnaburg fabric for towel, a 4" x 15" strip of fabric for trim at bottom of towel, a 1½" x 30" bias strip of fabric for trim strips, thread to match fabrics, and red, green, and brown acrylic paint.
For basket, you will need an approx. 9½" dia. basket with area suitable for stenciling, red and green acrylic paint, foam brush (optional), and a fabric square to line basket.

You will also need tracing paper, graphite transfer paper, tagboard (manila folder), craft knife, small stencil brushes, paper towels, removable tape (optional), and cutting mat or a thick layer of newspapers.

1. For towel, follow How To Stencil, page 122, to stencil design 1½" from 1 short edge (bottom) of towel fabric.
2. For trim at bottom of towel, match wrong sides and fold trim fabric in half lengthwise; press. With right sides facing, match long raw edge of trim to bottom raw edge of towel; use a ½" seam allowance to sew trim to towel. Press seam allowance toward top of towel.
3. For bias trim strips, press long raw edges of fabric strip ½" to wrong side; cut strip in half. Pin 1 strip ⅝" below stenciled design; pin remaining strip ¼" above design. Sew strips to towel along each long edge.
4. Press raw edges of towel ¼" to wrong side; press ¼" to wrong side again and stitch in place.
5. For basket, follow How To Stencil, page 122, to stencil 1 tree from house design on side of basket; repeat as desired. If desired, paint basket handle red; allow to dry.
6. Line basket with fabric square.

COTTAGE CAKE

During the holidays, delight a friend with an English Pound Cake delivered in a charming little cottage. Brandy and mace lend traditional British flavor to the cake. Cleverly crafted from a shoe box, the Dickensian cottage makes an engaging carrier for your gift. Your friend will enjoy displaying this wonderful accessory throughout the year!

ENGLISH POUND CAKE

  1 cup butter or margarine, softened
1½ cups granulated sugar
  5 eggs
  2 tablespoons brandy
1½ cups all-purpose flour
  2 teaspoons ground ginger
  1 teaspoon baking powder
  ½ teaspoon baking soda
  ½ teaspoon ground nutmeg
  ¼ teaspoon ground mace
  ¼ teaspoon salt

Preheat oven to 325 degrees. In a large bowl, cream butter and sugar until fluffy. Add eggs 1 at a time, beating well after each addition. Stir in brandy. In another large bowl, sift remaining ingredients together. Add dry ingredients to creamed mixture; beat until smooth. Pour batter into a greased and floured 5 x 9-inch loaf pan. Bake 1 hour 10 minutes to 1 hour 15 minutes or until a toothpick inserted in center comes out clean. Cool in pan 10 minutes; turn onto a wire rack to cool completely. Store in an airtight container.

Yield: about 15 servings

ENGLISH COUNTRY COTTAGE

You will need a shoe box (our shoe box measured 6″ x 11″ x 3½″), desired colors of Paper Capers™ twisted paper for walls and shingles, medium weight cardboard for side walls and roof, desired colors of mat board or painted lightweight cardboard for decorative details (windows, shutters, door, door hardware, or timber framing), craft knife, ⅛″ dia. bead for doorknob, a 1¼″ dia. artificial wreath, craft glue, and sheet moss.

Note: ''Paper'' in instructions refers to untwisted Paper Capers™.

1. Set aside box top to use for decorative details if desired. For side walls, measure height of 1 end of box and multiply by 2; measure width of end of box. Cut 2 pieces of medium weight cardboard the determined measurements.
2. For gable, mark center of each long edge of 1 side wall with a dot; mark center of 1 short edge of side wall with a dot. Draw lines from dot on each long edge to dot on short edge. Cut along marked lines. Matching remaining short edge of side wall to bottom edge of 1 end of box, glue side wall to box. Repeat for remaining side wall.
3. Cover house with paper, using glue to secure.
4. For roof, measure length of box and add 2″; measure width of box and multiply by 2. Cut a piece of medium weight cardboard the determined measurements. Fold cardboard in half lengthwise. Place roof on house; trim to desired size if necessary.
5. For shingles, cut approximately 1″ x 4″ strips of paper. Matching short edges, fold each strip in half, but do not crease. With each row overlapping the previous row, begin at bottom edge on each side of roof and glue rows of shingles to roof.
6. Cut decorative details (windows, shutters, door, door hardware, or timber framing) from mat board or painted cardboard; glue details to house. Glue bead to door for doorknob. Glue wreath to door. Glue pieces of sheet moss to roof. Allow to dry.
7. Place cake wrapped in plastic wrap in house. Place roof on house.

PISTACHIO TREASURE BOX

A treasure box filled with Pistachio Candy is a delicious way to pamper someone during the holidays. Wrapped in shimmering foil and delivered in our beautiful box, the candy makes an elegant gift. The "corsage" of porcelainized roses transforms the plain wicker box into an exquisite keepsake.

PISTACHIO CANDY

- 1 box (3 ounces) vanilla pudding mix (do not use instant)
- 1 cup granulated sugar
- 1 can (5 ounces) evaporated milk
- 2 tablespoons butter or margarine
- 1 tablespoon pistachio flavoring Green food coloring
- ½ cup chopped pistachios

In a medium saucepan, combine first 3 ingredients over medium heat and bring mixture to a boil. Continue to boil 5 minutes, stirring constantly. Remove from heat and stir in butter and pistachio flavoring. Tint to desired color. Pour mixture into a medium bowl. Beat at high speed with an electric mixer 4 to 5 minutes or until mixture thickens and is no longer glossy. Fold in pistachios. Spoon into greased candy molds. Refrigerate until firm. Remove candy from molds. Place 1 red and 1 gold foil candy wrapper wrong sides together and wrap each candy. Store in an airtight container in refrigerator.

Yield: about 4 dozen candies

ROSE TREASURE BOX

You will need a white oval wicker box with lid, 1 silk rose and 2 silk rosebuds with leaves, satin ribbon, Petal Porcelain™ setting agent, newspapers, Folk Art® Clearcote Extra Thick Glaze spray, hot glue gun, and glue sticks.

1. Remove roses and leaves from stems. Dip roses and leaves in setting agent; squeeze to remove excess. Hang roses and leaves upside down over newspapers and allow to dry.
2. Arrange roses and leaves on lid; glue to secure.
3. Apply 1 coat of glaze to roses and box; allow to dry.
4. Tie ribbon into a bow; glue bow to lid.

GLAD CHRISTMAS GREETINGS

*Y*ou'll send "Glad Christmas Greetings" when you present these yummy Lemon Ginger Cookies in our wooden keepsake box. A hint of lemon and a dusting of sugar give the spicy cookies a sweet citrusy flavor. The decoupage box, decorated with lovely old Christmas cards, can be used year after year to store holiday stationery, cards, or other special items.

LEMON GINGER COOKIES

2½ cups all-purpose flour
  1 tablespoon ground ginger
  2 teaspoons grated dried lemon peel
  2 teaspoons baking soda
  ½ teaspoon salt
  ½ teaspoon ground cinnamon
  ¼ teaspoon ground cloves
  ¼ teaspoon ground nutmeg
  ¾ cup butter or margarine, softened
  1 cup firmly packed brown sugar
  ¼ cup molasses
  1 egg
    Granulated sugar

Preheat oven to 350 degrees. In a large bowl, sift together first 8 ingredients. In another large bowl, cream butter and brown sugar until fluffy. Add molasses and egg; beat until smooth. Add dry ingredients; stir until a soft dough forms. Shape dough into 1-inch balls; roll each ball in sugar. Transfer cookies to a greased baking sheet. Bake 8 to 10 minutes or until light brown. Cool completely on a wire rack.

Store in an airtight container.

Yield: about 7 dozen cookies

CHRISTMAS CARD BOX

You will need a wooden box, metallic gold spray paint, matte Mod Podge® sealer, Christmas cards, ¼"w gold braid trim, and a foam brush.

1. Spray paint box gold; allow to dry.
2. Cut desired pictures and words from cards; arrange on box lid. Use sealer to glue cutouts to lid; allow to dry.
3. Apply 2 coats of sealer to lid, allowing to dry between coats.
4. Use sealer to glue braid along top edge of lid; allow to dry.

SANTA'S LAYERED FUDGE

This fudge is so good that everyone will think it's Santa's own recipe! The rich candy features layers of creamy chocolate and caramel fudge, so it's like two treats in one. Our jolly Santa is created by topping a basket with a drawstring bag. We "dressed" the old gentleman in a Christmas crazy-patch shirt sewn from festive fabrics.

CARAMEL-CHOCOLATE LAYERED FUDGE

CARAMEL FUDGE

2 cups granulated sugar
½ cup evaporated milk
5 tablespoons light corn syrup
3 tablespoons butter or margarine
1 tablespoon honey
¼ teaspoon salt
1 teaspoon vanilla extract
1 cup finely chopped walnuts

CHOCOLATE FUDGE

4 cups granulated sugar
1 cup evaporated milk
⅓ cup light corn syrup
6 tablespoons butter or margarine
2 tablespoons honey
½ teaspoon salt
1 teaspoon vanilla extract
1½ cups semisweet chocolate chips
1 cup finely chopped walnuts

For caramel fudge, grease sides of a large stockpot. Combine first 6 ingredients in stockpot and cook over medium-low heat, stirring constantly until sugar dissolves. Using a pastry brush dipped in hot water, wash down any sugar crystals on sides of stockpot. Attach candy thermometer to stockpot, making sure thermometer does not touch bottom of stockpot. Increase heat to medium and bring to a boil. Do not stir while syrup is boiling. Cook until syrup reaches soft ball stage (approximately 234 to 240 degrees). Test about ½ teaspoon syrup in ice water. Syrup should easily form a ball in ice water but flatten when held in your hand. Place stockpot in 2 inches of cold water in sink. Add vanilla; do not stir until syrup cools to approximately 110 degrees. Using medium speed of an electric mixer, beat fudge until it is no longer glossy and thickens. Pour into a greased 8 x 11-inch baking dish. Sprinkle walnuts evenly over.

For chocolate fudge, follow instructions for caramel fudge until syrup cools to approximately 110 degrees. Add chocolate chips and beat fudge using medium speed of an electric mixer until it is no longer glossy and thickens. Pour chocolate fudge over caramel fudge. Sprinkle walnuts evenly on top. Allow to harden. Cut into 1-inch squares. Store in an airtight container in refrigerator.

Yield: about 7 dozen squares fudge

SANTA BASKET

You will need a 6½″ dia. x 3½″h market basket with handle, two 6″ squares of muslin fabric for head, four 4″ x 9″ pieces of muslin fabric for arms, two 7″ x 9″ pieces of fabric for hat, a 7″ x 22″ piece of fabric for shirt, a 1⅝″ x 7″ strip of fabric for placket, two 7″ x 8″ pieces of fabric for sleeves, a 1⅝″ x 23″ strip of fabric for belt, thread to match fabrics, 1 yd of ¼″w ribbon, six ⅜″ dia. buttons, two 3⁄16″ dia. black doll eyes, fabric marking pencil, tracing paper, polyester fiberfill, heavy thread (buttonhole twist), seam ripper, 1 yd of curly wool roving for beard, 7″ of 32-gauge spool wire for glasses, craft glue, and powder blush.

1. Use head and arm patterns, page 66, and follow Transferring Patterns and Sewing Shapes, page 122, to make 1 head and 2 arms from fabric pieces. Stuff shapes with fiberfill; sew final closures by hand.
2. To make indentations for eyes, use heavy thread and come up through head at one ●; go down through head approximately ⅛″ away. Pull thread tightly to create a dimple in head; knot thread and trim ends. Repeat for remaining ●. Glue 1 doll eye in each indentation.
3. For cheeks, apply blush under eyes.
4. For beard, unbraid roving and cut into 3″ lengths. Glue roving along bottom ⅓ of face. Arrange beard as desired.
5. For glasses, refer to Fig. 1 and bend wire as shown to fit face. Glue ends of wire to head.

Fig. 1

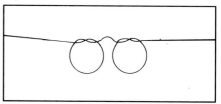

6. Leaving bottom edge open, use hat pattern, page 66, and follow Transferring Patterns and Sewing Shapes, page 122, to make hat from fabric pieces. Press bottom edge of hat ½″ to wrong side; glue to secure. Glue hat to head.
7. For placket on shirt, press long edges of fabric strip ½″ to wrong side. Center placket between short edges on right side of shirt fabric. Stitch close to long edges of placket to secure.
8. For shirt, match right sides and short edges and use a ½″ seam allowance to sew short edges of fabric together; press seam allowance open. For casing, press 1 raw edge (top) of shirt ¼″ to wrong side; press ¾″ to wrong side again. Stitch ⅝″ from top edge. Use seam ripper to open casing on inside of shirt at seamline. Thread ribbon through casing. Turn right side out. Spacing evenly, sew 4 buttons to placket.
9. For sleeves, match right sides and fold 1 sleeve piece in half lengthwise. Using a ½″ seam allowance, sew along long edge and 1 short edge. Press

Continued on page 66

SANTA BASKET (continued)

remaining raw edge 1½″ to wrong side. Clip corners and turn right side out. Repeat for remaining sleeve.

10. Insert 1 arm into 1 sleeve. Fold sleeve at wrist as shown in Fig. 2. Sew 1 button to sleeve over folds. Tack sleeve to wrist. Repeat for remaining arm.

Fig. 2

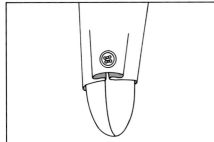

11. Whipstitch head to casing at center front of shirt. Being careful not to catch ribbon in stitching, whipstitch 1 sleeve to casing 2″ from each side of placket.

12. With arms placed over basket handle, place shirt over top of basket. With bottom edge of shirt overlapping basket rim ½″, glue edge of shirt to basket rim, easing to fit if necessary.

13. For belt, press edges of fabric strip ½″ to wrong side. Overlapping ends in back, glue belt to rim of basket, covering raw edges of shirt.

14. Place a plastic bag of fudge in basket. Pull ribbon ends to close top of shirt; tie ends into a bow.

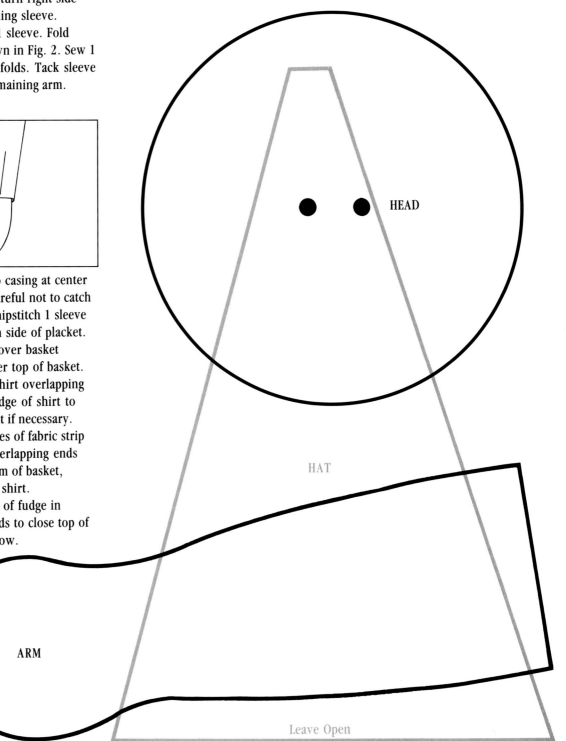

A "SOUP-R" GIFT

*O*n a frosty day, a friend will appreciate the thoughtful warmth of this "soup-r" gift. Our spicy Black Bean Soup features a hearty combination of beans, rice, carrots, and bacon, and the Christmas Pepper Relish is a perfect complement. A stockpot can serve as a convenient carrier for your gift. Just for fun, wrap a cheerful muffler around the pot — it'll make a festive table runner to warm up any winter meal!

BLACK BEAN SOUP

    1   package (16 ounces) dried black
          beans
   10   cups water
    8   slices bacon
    1   can (10½ ounces) chicken broth
    3   large carrots, finely chopped
    1   large onion, finely chopped
    2   tablespoons garlic powder
    1   tablespoon salt
    1   teaspoon ground cumin
    1   teaspoon ground black pepper
    1   cup cooked rice

In a large stockpot, soak beans in water 8 hours or overnight. In a small skillet, cook bacon until crisp, drain on paper towels, and crumble. Add bacon and next 7 ingredients to beans; mix well. Bring to a boil over medium-high heat. Reduce heat to medium, cover, and simmer 3 hours or until beans are soft. Remove from heat; stir in rice. Store in an airtight container in refrigerator. Give with instructions for reheating.

To reheat, transfer soup to a large stockpot. Cook over medium heat 10 to 15 minutes or until heated through. Serve hot with Christmas Pepper Relish (recipe follows).

Yield: about 8 cups soup

CHRISTMAS PEPPER RELISH

   ½   cup chopped sweet red pepper
   ½   cup chopped green pepper
   ¼   cup diced onion
   1   teaspoon apple cider vinegar
   1   teaspoon garlic powder
   1   teaspoon salt
   ½   teaspoon dried oregano
   ½   teaspoon crushed bay leaves
   ½   teaspoon ground black pepper

Combine all ingredients in a small bowl; stir until well blended. Cover and chill 8 hours or overnight to allow flavors to blend. Store in an airtight container in refrigerator. Serve with Black Bean Soup.

Yield: about 1 cup relish

HEAVENLY MORSELS

These heavenly *Caramelized Cake Squares* are so delicious that no one will believe how easy they are to make! They're created by dipping bits of light, fluffy angel food cake into caramel and then rolling them in nuts. A paper bag spritzed with gold paint and adorned with our lacy angel is a grand way to present the candy-like morsels. Crafted from paper doilies, the sweet angel makes a divine tree ornament later.

CARAMELIZED CAKE SQUARES

- 2 cups butter or margarine
- 2 cups firmly packed brown sugar
- 1 purchased angel food cake (7-inch diameter), cut into 1-inch cubes
- 4 cups finely chopped pecans

In a large saucepan, combine butter and sugar over medium heat, stirring constantly until sugar dissolves. Bring to a boil and cook until syrup reaches soft ball stage (234 to 240 degrees); remove from heat. Using tongs, dip cake cubes in syrup; roll in pecans. Place on waxed paper to cool completely. Store in an airtight container.

Yield: about 5 dozen cake squares

ANGEL ORNAMENT

For ornament, you will need two 5″ dia. paper doilies, 1½ yds of yellow cotton yarn, 4″ of ⅛″ dia. gold cord, 8″ of metallic gold thread, craft glue, Design Master® glossy wood tone spray (available at craft stores), tracing paper, medium weight cardboard, peach acrylic paint, paintbrush, black permanent felt-tip pen with fine point, red colored pencil, and a sprig of artificial holly.
For bag, you will need desired paper bag, gold spray paint, ⅛″ dia. gold cord, and hole punch.

1. (*Note:* Allow to dry after each glue step.) For body, refer to Fig. 1 and roll 1 doily into a cone shape; glue overlapping edges to secure. Flatten cone slightly. Trace base pattern onto tracing paper; cut out. Use pattern and cut 1 base from cardboard. Matching point of base to point of cone, glue base over overlapped area of cone (back).

Fig. 1

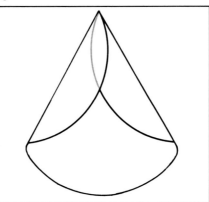

2. Cut remaining doily in half.
3. For arms, cut 1 half of doily in half again. Overlap straight edges and roll 1 doily piece into a cone shape; glue to secure. Repeat with remaining doily piece. Glue arms to body front.
4. For wings, cut remaining half of doily into thirds; discard 1 piece. Glue 1 doily piece to back of body for each wing.

5. For head, cut a 1¼″ dia. circle from cardboard. Paint circle peach; allow to dry. Use pen to draw eyes and mouth on circle; use red pencil to color cheeks.
6. For hair, cut ten 5″ lengths of yarn. Spray lightly with wood tone spray; allow to dry. Center and glue 9 lengths along top of head. For bangs, form loops with remaining length; glue to center top of head.
7. For halo, form cord into a circle. Glue ends to back of head. Glue head to top of body. Glue holly sprig below 1 sleeve.
8. For hanger, knot ends of metallic thread together. Glue knot to back of head.
9. For bag, lightly spray paint bag gold; allow to dry. Place a plastic bag of cake squares in bag. Fold top of bag down 2″. Punch 2 holes through folded portion of bag. Thread cord through holes and tie into a bow. Loop angel ornament hanger around bow.

BASE

A Sweet Surprise

Dressed up for the holidays, a festive jar of Peppermint Marmalade will be a sweet surprise for a special family! Just the right combination of citrus and fresh mint lends a cool flavor to the jelly. Served on biscuits or English muffins, it's sure to be a hit. With a little doorknob basket, you can deliver the treat secretly — just like Santa's elves!

PEPPERMINT MARMALADE

- 4 cups firmly packed fresh mint leaves
- 3¼ cups water, divided
- 1 medium orange
- 1 medium lemon
- 1 can (6 ounces) frozen pineapple juice concentrate, thawed
- 3¾ cups granulated sugar
- 1 box (1¾ ounces) fruit pectin
- 1 teaspoon mint extract

In a medium saucepan, combine mint leaves and 2½ cups water. Cover and bring to a boil over high heat. Reduce heat to medium; simmer 30 minutes. Remove from heat; cool to room temperature. Chill 8 hours or overnight. Strain mint mixture into a large bowl. Reserve 2 cups mint water; discard leaves.

Peel orange and lemon; cut peels into very thin strips. Place peels and remaining water in a large saucepan; bring to a boil over high heat. Reduce heat to medium-low, cover, and simmer 10 minutes, stirring occasionally. Finely chop fruit pulp and discard seeds. Add fruit, pineapple juice, and reserved mint water to peel mixture. Cover and simmer 12 minutes longer. Add sugar and pectin and bring to boil over medium-high heat. Boil 1 minute, stirring constantly. Remove from heat. Stir in mint extract. Skim foam from top of marmalade. Following Sealing Jars instructions, page 120, pour into sterilized jars. Store in refrigerator.

Yield: about 2 pints marmalade

PEPPERMINT BASKET

You will need a 1 pint canning jar with lid, an approx. 4" x 4" x 4" basket with hanging loop, one 4" fabric square for jar lid insert, 20" of ⅛"w ribbon, one 1¾" x 18" fabric strip for basket trim, lightweight cardboard, craft batting, and craft glue.

1. For jar lid insert, use flat part of lid as a pattern and cut 1 circle each from cardboard, batting, and fabric.
2. Matching edges, glue batting to cardboard. Center fabric circle on batting; glue edge of fabric to batting.
3. Follow Sealing Jars instructions, page 120, to place jar lid insert into screw ring.
4. Tie ribbon into a bow around lid.
5. For basket trim, press edges of fabric strip ½" to wrong side. With wrong side of strip facing basket rim, glue strip to rim.
6. Place jar in basket.

FELIZ NAVIDAD

*Y*our friends will say *"Olé!"* when you deliver this spicy holiday treat! Presented in a basket with a festive fabric liner, our Cumin Bread lends a Southwestern taste to the Yuletide celebration. For extra South-of-the-Border style, send along a cactus all decked out for Christmas!

CUMIN BREAD

    3   cups all-purpose flour
    ¼   cup granulated sugar
    2   tablespoons baking powder
    4   teaspoons ground cumin
    2   teaspoons salt
    1   teaspoon cumin seed, crushed
    ½   teaspoon dry mustard
    3   eggs
 1½   cups milk
    ⅓   cup vegetable oil
    3   tablespoons picante sauce

Preheat oven to 350 degrees. In a large bowl, combine first 7 ingredients. In a medium bowl, whisk together remaining ingredients. Add egg mixture to dry ingredients; stir just until batter is moist. Pour batter evenly into 3 greased 3 x 5½-inch loaf pans. Bake 25 to 30 minutes or until a toothpick inserted in center comes out clean. Cool in pans 10 minutes; turn onto a wire rack to cool completely. Store in an airtight container. Give with instructions to serve.

Bread may be served at room temperature or warm. To reheat, preheat oven to 350 degrees. Bake uncovered on an ungreased baking sheet 3 to 5 minutes or until heated through.

Yield: 3 loaves bread

Winter Warmer

A *steaming pot of home-cooked soup made with our spicy Curry Soup Mix is a flavorful way to warm up on a cold winter's day. To share the warmth with a friend, give the dry mix — a blend of rice, nuts, and seasonings — along with instructions for making the soup. Your friend can add cooked chicken or shrimp to make a hearty one-dish meal. A pretty basket trimmed with ribbon and greenery makes a nice container for a bag of the mix and a pair of soup mugs. When the soup is gone, the basket can be used to display Christmas cards or other holiday accents.*

Curry Soup Mix

    2 cups uncooked instant rice
    ½ cup raisins
    ⅓ cup chopped walnuts
    ¼ cup dried minced onions
    2 tablespoons salt
    1 tablespoon curry powder
    1 tablespoon granulated sugar
    2 teaspoons paprika
 1 ½ teaspoons dried dill weed
    1 teaspoon dry mustard
    1 teaspoon ground coriander
    1 teaspoon garlic powder
    ½ teaspoon ground cardamom

In a large bowl, combine all ingredients, stirring until well blended. Store in an airtight container. Give with instructions for making soup.

To make soup, bring 10 cups water to a boil in a large stockpot over high heat; add soup mix. Cover and reduce heat to medium. Stirring occasionally, simmer 20 to 25 minutes or until rice is tender. Stir in about 2 cups shredded cooked chicken or cooked peeled shrimp; cook until heated through. Serve immediately. Store in an airtight container in refrigerator.

Yield: 6 to 8 servings

For fabric bag, cut a 7" x 30" piece of fabric and follow Steps 2 and 4 of Fabric Bag instructions, page 123. Press top edge of bag 3" to wrong side. Place a plastic bag of soup mix in bag. Tie a 20" length of ribbon into a bow around top of bag. Tuck a sprig of artificial holly behind bow.

CAJUN CHRISTMAS

Give a taste of Louisiana this Christmas with a Cajun barbecue basket! Our chunky Apricot Barbecue Sauce lends sweet, spicy flavor to grilled meats, and chopped walnuts and cayenne pepper make the hot, tangy Cajun Coleslaw a special treat. Cotton bolls and a pillow ticking liner add Southern charm to the festive basket. To complete your gift, include a handful of mesquite chips and a bundle of long matches for outdoor cooking.

CAJUN COLESLAW

1 small head green cabbage, shredded
1 cup chopped walnuts
¾ cup mayonnaise
¼ cup red wine vinegar
3 tablespoons Dijon-style mustard
2 teaspoons garlic powder
1 teaspoon ground cayenne pepper

In a large bowl, combine cabbage and walnuts. In a small bowl, whisk together remaining ingredients. Pour mayonnaise mixture over cabbage mixture; stir until well blended. Cover and refrigerate 2 to 3 hours to allow flavors to blend. Store in an airtight container in refrigerator.

Yield: about 6 servings

APRICOT BARBECUE SAUCE

¼ cup vegetable oil
1 small onion, finely chopped
1 package (6 ounces) dried apricots
2 tablespoons granulated sugar
½ cup ketchup
½ cup water
¼ cup red wine vinegar
1 teaspoon ground oregano
1 teaspoon ground cayenne pepper
1 teaspoon salt
1 teaspoon hot pepper sauce
½ teaspoon Worcestershire sauce

In a large saucepan, combine oil and onion. Sauté onion over medium heat, stirring occasionally until onion is soft. In a blender or food processor fitted with a steel blade, process apricots and sugar until finely chopped. Stir apricot mixture and remaining ingredients into onion mixture; bring to a boil. Boil 3 to 5 minutes, stirring occasionally until sauce thickens. Store in an airtight container in refrigerator. Serve warm with meat.

Yield: about 2 cups sauce

For basket, wrap basket handle with stems of artificial cotton bolls, preserved cedar, dried red canella berries, and strands of red raffia; hot glue to secure. Cut a fabric square for liner; fringe edges ½". Place liner in basket and fill basket with mesquite chips. Tie red raffia around a bundle of long matches; place in basket.

Topped with snowy drifts of fluffy frosting, our luscious Coconut Cream Cake looks like a delightful winter wonderland! To surprise a friend, send a trio of playful papier mâché penguins along with the snowcapped cake. Even when the cake is gone, they'll make adorable sit-abouts or ornaments.

COCONUT CREAM CAKE

CAKE

- 1 cup butter or margarine, softened
- 2 cups granulated sugar
- 5 eggs
- 1 teaspoon vanilla extract
- 2 cups all-purpose flour
- 1 teaspoon baking soda
- ½ teaspoon salt
- 1 cup buttermilk
- 2 cups sweetened shredded coconut
- 1 cup finely chopped pecans

FROSTING

- 2 cups whipping cream
- ⅓ cup granulated sugar
- ⅓ cup sour cream
- 3 cups sweetened shredded coconut, divided

Preheat oven to 350 degrees. For cake, cream butter and sugar in a large bowl until fluffy. Add eggs 1 at a time, beating well after each addition. Stir in vanilla. In another large bowl, sift together next 3 ingredients. Stir dry ingredients and buttermilk alternately into creamed mixture. Fold in coconut and pecans. Pour batter into 3 greased and floured 9-inch round cake pans. Bake 30 to 35 minutes or until a toothpick inserted in center comes out clean. Cool in pan 10 minutes; turn onto a wire rack to cool completely.

For frosting, whip cream in a chilled large bowl until soft peaks form. Add sugar and sour cream; beat until stiff peaks form. Fold in 2 cups coconut. Spread about ⅓ cup frosting between layers of cake. Spread remaining frosting on sides and top of cake. Sprinkle remaining coconut on top and sides of cake.

Yield: about 20 servings

PENGUIN ORNAMENTS

For each ornament, you will need one 2½″ long papier mâché egg (available at craft stores); white, dk yellow, orange, and black acrylic paint; foam brush; paintbrushes; tracing paper; lightweight cardboard; two 5″ squares of red flannel fabric for hat; fabric marking pencil; small crochet hook (for turning fabric); one ½″ dia. white pom-pom; 2″ of ¼″w red satin ribbon; red thread; hot glue gun; and glue sticks.

1. Paint egg black. Allow to dry.
2. Use a pencil to sketch body pattern onto egg.
3. (*Note:* Allow to dry after each paint color.) Paint shirt and eyes white, buttons black, and nose orange.
4. Trace foot and hat patterns onto tracing paper; cut out.
5. Use foot pattern and cut 2 feet from cardboard. Paint feet dk yellow; allow to dry. Overlapping round ends of feet, glue feet to bottom of egg.
6. For hat, leave bottom edge open and follow Sewing Shapes, page 122, to make hat from fabric squares. Press bottom edge ¼″ to wrong side; glue to secure. Glue pom-pom to point of hat. Glue hat to penguin. Fold hat to 1 side; glue in place.
7. For tie, wrap thread around center of ribbon and knot ends together. Cut a V-shaped notch in each end of ribbon. Glue tie to penguin.

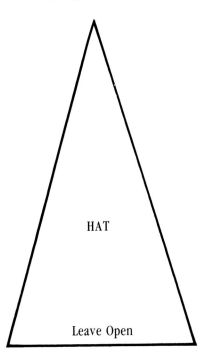

HAT

Leave Open

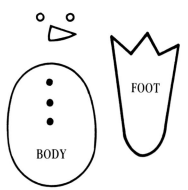

BODY

FOOT

ELEGANT BREAKFAST LOAF

*F*illed with cream cheese and festive red cherries, a loaf of Cherry Swirl Bread makes a scrumptious addition to a holiday breakfast or brunch. A light glaze and a hint of orange lend richness to the sweet yeast bread. For an elegant presentation, line a decorated bread basket with a doily of Battenburg lace.

CHERRY SWIRL BREAD

BREAD

- 3½ cups all-purpose flour, divided
- ⅓ cup granulated sugar
- ¾ teaspoon salt
- 2 packages active dry yeast
- ½ cup butter or margarine, softened
- ¼ cup milk
- ½ cup water
- 1 egg

FILLING

- 1 cup dried pitted cherries
- 1 cup water
- 2 packages (8 ounces each) cream cheese, softened
- ⅔ cup confectioners sugar
- 1 tablespoon grated dried orange peel
- 2 egg yolks, beaten

GLAZE

- 1 cup confectioners sugar
- 2 tablespoons butter or margarine, melted
- 2 tablespoons milk

For bread, combine 1 cup flour and next 3 ingredients in a large bowl. In a medium saucepan, combine butter, milk and water over low heat. Stir until mixture reaches approximately 130 degrees on a candy thermometer (butter may not be completely melted). Add butter mixture to dry ingredients. Mix with an electric mixer at medium speed about 2 minutes or until well blended. Add egg; beat until smooth. Gradually add remaining flour, kneading until a soft dough forms. Turn dough onto a lightly floured surface; continue to knead about 8 minutes or until dough is pliable and elastic. Shape dough into a ball; transfer to a greased bowl. Grease top of dough and cover. Let rise in a warm place (80 to 85 degrees) 1 hour or until doubled in size.

For filling, soak cherries in 1 cup water 2 hours; drain well. In a medium bowl, combine remaining ingredients; beat until smooth. Fold in cherries.

Divide dough in half. Turn half of dough onto a lightly floured surface and use a floured rolling pin to roll out dough to a 9 x 13-inch rectangle. Spread half of filling evenly on rectangle to within 1 inch of edges. Beginning with 1 long edge, roll dough jelly-roll fashion. Transfer to a greased baking sheet. Tuck ends of dough under. Cut slashes on top of dough about 2 inches apart. Repeat for remaining dough. Cover and let rise in a warm place 1 hour or until doubled in size.

Preheat oven to 350 degrees. Bake bread 30 to 35 minutes or until golden brown. For glaze, whisk all ingredients together in a small bowl. Brush hot bread with glaze. Cool completely on a wire rack. Store in an airtight container. Give with instructions for reheating.

To reheat, preheat oven to 350 degrees. Bake uncovered on an ungreased baking sheet 5 to 8 minutes or until heated through.

Yield: 2 loaves bread

GRACEFUL GOBLETS

Sparkling jelly given in graceful goblets is an elegant holiday offering for a special friend. Made with red wine, the gourmet treat has a fruity flavor that's delicious on hot breads or with cream cheese and crackers. For a lovely presentation, choose a handsome set of wineglasses and fill one or all with the jelly. Holiday gift wrap and a pretty bow transform the carton into a beautiful gift box to hold the sweet surprise.

WINE JELLY

  2 cups red Zinfandel wine
  6 cups granulated sugar
  1 box (1¾ ounces) fruit pectin

Combine wine and sugar in a large stockpot over medium heat, stirring constantly until sugar dissolves. Increase heat to medium-high and bring to a boil. Add pectin; stir well. Bring to a rolling boil and boil 1 minute longer; remove from heat. Skim off foam. Fill wine glasses ⅔ full. Follow Sealing With Paraffin instructions, page 120, to seal glasses. Store in refrigerator.

Yield: about 2 pints jelly

For box, follow Gift Box 2 instructions, page 123. We covered the box our wine glasses were purchased in and decorated it with ⅞" wide ribbon.

With a name like Trash Snack Mix, kids will never guess that this yummy treat is good for them! Packed with oats, nuts, raisins, and other healthy ingredients, the honey-sweetened mix is sure to be a hit. It makes an irresistible gift when presented in a ''chimney'' topped with a lovable Santa hand puppet.

TRASH SNACK MIX

- 1 cup toasted oat cereal
- 1 cup old-fashioned rolled oats
- ½ cup shredded coconut
- ½ cup whole unsalted almonds
- ½ cup wheat germ
- ½ cup shelled unsalted sunflower seeds
- ½ cup raisins
- ½ cup honey
- ¼ cup light corn syrup
- ¼ cup vegetable oil
- 1 teaspoon vanilla extract
- 1 teaspoon almond extract

Preheat oven to 325 degrees. In a large bowl, stir together first 7 ingredients. In a medium bowl, use medium speed of an electric mixer to beat remaining ingredients until well blended. Pour honey mixture over dry ingredients, stirring until well coated. Spread evenly on a greased baking sheet. Bake 20 to 25 minutes or until brown. Cool completely in pan. Break into pieces. Store in an airtight container.

Yield: about 5½ cups snack mix

SANTA HAND PUPPET

You will need the following pieces of felt: two 8½" x 11" pieces of red, one 8½" x 11" piece of white, one 6" square of green, one 3" square of pink, and one ¾" x 9¾" strip of black; tracing paper; removable fabric marking pen; 6" of ⅛"w flat gold braid; one ⅜" dia. red pom-pom; one 1" dia. white pom-pom; two ³⁄₁₆" dia. black beads; red thread; washable fabric glue; craft glue; polyester fiberfill; craft knife; a 4¼" x 4¼" x 5¼" boutique tissue box; black and copper spray paint; sandpaper; utility scissors; and one 6" square of ⅜" thick plastic foam.

1. (*Note:* Use fabric glue to assemble puppet.) Matching registration marks (⊕) and overlapping pattern parts, trace body pattern, page 80, onto tracing paper; cut out. Trace remaining patterns, page 80, onto tracing paper; cut out.
2. Matching edges, place red felt pieces together. Center body pattern on felt pieces; use fabric marking pen to draw around pattern. Leaving bottom edge open, sew pieces together directly on pen line. Cutting close to stitching line, cut out body. Remove pen lines.
3. Use patterns and cut 1 face piece from pink felt, 1 beard piece and 1 mustache piece from white felt, and 4 mitten pieces from green felt.
4. Cut one ⅝" x 6¼" strip from white felt for hat trim; cut two ⅜" x 3⅝" strips from white felt for mitten trim.
5. With straight edge (top) 2" from top of body, glue face piece to body front. Matching straight edges at top of beard piece to top of face piece, glue beard piece over face piece. With ends of hat trim strip at back of body and 1 long edge overlapping top edges of face and beard pieces ¼", glue hat trim strip to

body. Glue mustache over beard. Allow to dry.
6. Matching edges, glue 1 mitten piece to front and back of each hand. With ends of each mitten trim strip at back of body and 1 long edge overlapping bottom edges of mitten pieces ⅛", glue mitten trim strips to body. Allow to dry.
7. For belt, place black felt strip with ends at back of body and 1 long edge 3¼" from bottom edge of body; glue to secure. For buckle, cut two 1¼" pieces and two 1⅜" pieces from gold braid. Using short pieces for sides of buckle and long pieces for top and bottom of buckle, glue braid to puppet. Allow to dry.
8. Glue red pom-pom to center of mustache for nose. Glue white pom-pom to hat. Glue beads to face for eyes. Allow to dry.
9. (*Note:* Use craft glue to assemble chimney.) For chimney, cut top from tissue box. Spray paint box black. Allow to dry.
10. Cut two 1¼" x 4¼" strips and two 1¼" x 5" strips from plastic foam. Glue short strips to opposite sides of box along top edge. Glue long strips to remaining sides of box. Allow to dry.
11. For bricks, use utility scissors to cut ¾" x 2" pieces from sandpaper; round off corners of pieces. Spray paint some of the pieces with a light coat and some with a medium coat of copper paint; allow to dry. Glue to sides of box; allow to dry.
12. Stuff top half of puppet lightly with fiberfill. Place a plastic bag of snack mix in bottom half of puppet. Place puppet in chimney. Remove fiberfill before playing with puppet.

Continued on page 80

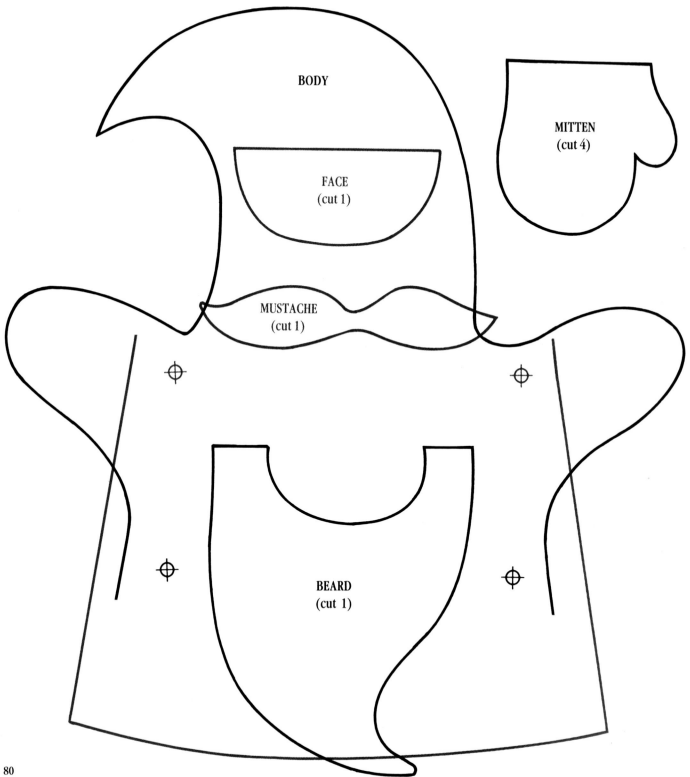

BODY

MITTEN
(cut 4)

FACE
(cut 1)

MUSTACHE
(cut 1)

BEARD
(cut 1)

REFRESHING GOODNESS

During the hectic holiday season, someone who's on the go will appreciate a quick, no-fuss meal. Light, refreshing Garden Gazpacho is served chilled, so it's especially easy — and it's nutritious, too! Tomato, cucumber, onion, and green pepper lend fresh garden goodness to the tangy soup. A basket dressed up with silk greenery will help you deliver your gift in festive style.

GARDEN GAZPACHO

1 can (10½ ounces) chicken broth
2 tablespoons apple cider vinegar
2 tablespoons vegetable oil
2 teaspoons salt
1 teaspoon granulated sugar
1 teaspoon garlic powder
1 teaspoon hot pepper sauce
1 teaspoon ground black pepper
½ teaspoon celery seed
4 large tomatoes, peeled and seeded
2 cucumbers, peeled and seeded
1 large onion
1 green pepper, seeded

Combine first 9 ingredients in a large bowl; stir until well blended. Coarsely chop remaining ingredients. In a food processor fitted with a steel blade, process vegetables until finely chopped. Stir into broth mixture. Cover and chill 8 hours or overnight to allow flavors to blend. Store in an airtight container in refrigerator. Serve chilled.

Yield: about 6 servings

GOURMET POPCORN

These gourmet seasonings are perfect for a popcorn lover. Mixed with melted butter and poured over freshly popped corn, the Parmesan-Garlic Popcorn Spice adds zest and the Chocolate-Cinnamon Popcorn Spice makes a sweet change of pace. Presented in a painted "popcorn" bowl filled with fluffy popcorn, the seasonings will suit anyone's tastes. Don't forget to give the serving instructions!

CHOCOLATE-CINNAMON POPCORN SPICE

½ cup confectioners sugar
¼ cup semisweet chocolate chips, chilled and finely ground
1 tablespoon plus 2 teaspoons cocoa
½ teaspoon ground cinnamon

Combine all ingredients in a small bowl; stir until well blended. Store in an airtight container. Give with instructions for serving.

To serve, melt ¼ cup butter in a small saucepan over low heat. Stir in 2 tablespoons popcorn spice. Pour over 3 cups popped corn; stir well.

Yield: about ¾ cup popcorn spice

PARMESAN-GARLIC POPCORN SPICE

½ cup grated Parmesan cheese
2 teaspoons salt
1 teaspoon dried tarragon
1 teaspoon garlic powder
1 teaspoon parsley flakes

Combine all ingredients in a small bowl; stir until well blended. Store in an airtight container. Give with instructions for serving.

To serve, melt ¼ cup butter in a small saucepan over low heat. Stir in 1 tablespoon popcorn spice. Pour over 3 cups popped corn; stir well.

Yield: about ½ cup popcorn spice

POPCORN BOWL

You will need a plastic bowl, easel green Design Master® Color Tool™ Enamel spray paint, and shiny butterscotch Scribbles® 3-Dimensional Fabric Writer.

Note: Bowl is for decorative use and should only be used for dry foods. Wipe clean with a damp cloth.

1. Spray paint bowl green; allow to dry.
2. Use fabric writer to paint "popcorn," holly leaves, and berries on bowl; allow to dry.

Tasty Trees

A basket of peppy tree-shaped Corn Bread Muffins makes a cute holiday gift! Loaded with sausage, corn, cheese, and peppers, the muffins are perfect for serving with hearty country meals. For delivery, perch a Christmasy bird on a basket lined with a fringed gingham cloth.

Corn Bread Muffins

- ½ pound mild pork sausage
- ¾ cup cornmeal
- ¼ cup all-purpose flour
- 1 tablespoon baking powder
- 1 teaspoon salt
- 2 eggs
- 1 cup sour cream
- ¾ cup butter or margarine, softened
- 1 teaspoon hot pepper sauce
- 1 package (10 ounces) frozen corn, thawed
- 1 cup (4 ounces) grated sharp Cheddar cheese
- ½ cup chopped sweet red pepper

Preheat oven to 375 degrees. In a large skillet, brown sausage over medium-high heat; drain well. In a large bowl, combine next 4 ingredients. Stir in next 4 ingredients; beat until smooth. Fold in sausage and remaining ingredients. Spoon batter into greased tree-shaped baking tins, filling tins ⅔ full. Bake 25 to 30 minutes or until a toothpick inserted in center comes out clean. Cool completely on a wire rack. Store in an airtight container. Give with instructions for reheating.

To reheat, preheat oven to 350 degrees. Bake on an ungreased baking sheet 8 to 10 minutes or until heated through.

Yield: about 1½ dozen 4-inch muffins

For bread cloth, cut desired size fabric square. Use 3 strands of coordinating floss and a long running stitch to stitch ¾" from edges of fabric square. Fringe edges of fabric square ½".

CHRISTMAS COOKIE CRATE

This Christmas cookie crate makes a nice gift for someone who enjoys holiday baking. By adding different ingredients to the basic Cookie Starter, your friend can create three scrumptious kinds of cookies! Present the mix along with the recipes and supplies for making Granola, Chocolate Chip, and Peanut Butter Cookies. Decorated with quilt-inspired friendship stars pieced from country fabrics, a wooden fruit crate is just right for delivering your gift.

COOKIE STARTER

4½ cups all-purpose flour
2 cups granulated sugar
2 cups firmly packed brown sugar
1½ cups nonfat dry milk
1 tablespoon plus 1 teaspoon salt
1½ cups shortening

In a very large bowl, combine first 5 ingredients. Using a pastry blender or 2 knives, cut in shortening until mixture resembles coarse meal. Store in an airtight container in refrigerator. Mix may be stored up to 6 months in the freezer. Give with recipes for Chocolate Chip, Peanut Butter, and Granola Cookies.

Yield: about 11½ cups cookie starter

GRANOLA COOKIES

1 cup Cookie Starter
1 cup granola cereal
1½ teaspoons ground cinnamon
1 egg
1 teaspoon vanilla extract
½ cup raisins

Preheat oven to 350 degrees. In a large bowl, mix together first 3 ingredients. Add egg and vanilla; stir until smooth. Fold in raisins. Drop by teaspoonfuls onto a greased baking sheet. Bake 10 to 12 minutes or until brown. Cool completely on a wire rack. Store in an airtight container.

Yield: about 2½ dozen cookies

PEANUT BUTTER COOKIES

1 cup crunchy peanut butter
1 egg
1 tablespoon water
1 teaspoon vanilla extract
1½ cups Cookie Starter

Preheat oven to 375 degrees. In a large bowl, combine first 4 ingredients;

beat until smooth. Add Cookie Starter; stir until a soft dough forms. Drop by teaspoonfuls onto a greased baking sheet. Bake 10 to 12 minutes or until brown. Cool completely on a wire rack. Store in an airtight container.

Yield: about 3 dozen cookies

CHOCOLATE CHIP COOKIES

½ cup butter or margarine, softened
1 egg
1 teaspoon vanilla extract
3 cups Cookie Starter
1 cup (6 ounces) semisweet chocolate chips
½ cup chopped pecans

Preheat oven to 350 degrees. In a large bowl, beat butter until fluffy. Add egg and vanilla; beat until smooth. Add Cookie Starter; stir until a soft dough forms. Fold in chocolate chips and pecans. Drop by teaspoonfuls onto a greased baking sheet. Bake 8 to 10 minutes or until brown. Cool completely on a wire rack. Store in an airtight container.

Yield: about 3 dozen cookies

FRIENDSHIP STAR COOKIE CRATE

You will need a wooden fruit crate (we found our 19½" x 12" x 6" crate in the produce department of a grocery store), desired fabrics for quilt blocks, medium weight fusible interfacing, paper-backed fusible web, tracing paper, parchment paper, black felt-tip

pen with fine point, ¹⁄₁₆" thick basswood (available at craft stores), utility scissors, Design Master® glossy wood tone spray (available at craft stores), and craft glue.

1. (*Note:* Follow Steps 1 - 7 for each 5⅛" block.) Cut a 6" square from 1 fabric. Cut a piece of interfacing slightly smaller than fabric square. Follow manufacturer's instructions to fuse interfacing to wrong side of fabric square. Cut a 5⅛" square from interfaced fabric.
2. Trace block pattern onto tracing paper; cut out. Use pattern and cut 1 block from parchment paper. Use pen to draw dashed lines around star to resemble stitches. Matching edges, glue parchment block to right side of interfaced fabric square.
3. Cut a 2" square from a second fabric; cut a 1½" square from a third fabric. Cut a piece of web slightly smaller than each fabric square. Follow manufacturer's instructions to fuse web to wrong side of each square.
4. Cut a 1¼" square from 2" fabric square. Fuse square to center of block.
5. Trace heart, tree, or star pattern onto tracing paper; cut out. Use pattern and cut shape from 1½" fabric square. Fuse shape to center of block.
6. Glue block to crate.
7. Cut two ⅝" x 3⅞" strips and two ⅝" x 5⅛" strips from basswood. Spray each strip lightly with wood tone spray; allow to dry. Glue strips around edges of block.

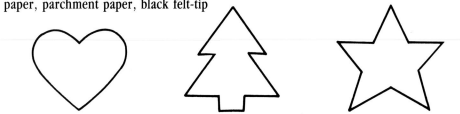

HOLIDAY BISCUITS

Rolled inside our hearty Peppered Cheese Biscuits, thinly sliced ham is a tasty surprise! Perfect for serving with breakfast or as appetizers, the biscuits make a savory holiday gift. To present them, line a basket with a cross-stitched bread cloth adorned with a pair of cheery redbirds.

PEPPERED CHEESE BISCUITS

- ⅔ cup grated Parmesan cheese
- 1½ teaspoons black pepper
- 2 cups all-purpose flour
- 1 tablespoon baking powder
- 1 teaspoon baking soda
- ½ teaspoon salt
- ⅛ teaspoon cayenne pepper
- 1 teaspoon dried minced onion
- ¼ cup butter or margarine, chilled and cut into small pieces
- ⅔ cup sour cream
- ⅓ cup half and half
- ½ pound thinly sliced deli ham
- 2 tablespoons butter or margarine, melted

Preheat oven to 450 degrees. Place cheese and black pepper in a blender or food processor fitted with a steel blade. Process 5 to 10 seconds or until finely ground. In a large bowl, sift together next 5 ingredients. Stir in cheese mixture and onion. Using a pastry blender or 2 knives, cut ¼ cup butter into dry ingredients until mixture resembles coarse meal. Stir in sour cream and half and half; knead until a soft dough forms. On a lightly floured surface, use a floured rolling pin to roll out dough to a ¼-inch thick rectangle. Place 1 layer of ham on dough. Beginning with 1 long edge, roll dough jelly-roll fashion. Wrap in plastic wrap and chill 1 hour.

Using a sharp knife, cut roll into ½-inch thick slices. Transfer to a greased baking sheet. Brush with melted butter. Bake 10 to 12 minutes or until brown. Cool completely on a wire rack. Store in an airtight container. Give with instructions for reheating.

To reheat, preheat oven to 350 degrees. Bake uncovered 2 to 3 minutes or until heated through.

Yield: about 2 dozen biscuits

BREAD CLOTH

You will need a Deep Teal Royal Classic bread cloth (14 ct), embroidery floss (see color key), and embroidery hoop (optional).

With bottom of design centered 1⅛" from 1 edge of bread cloth, work design on bread cloth using 2 strands of floss for all stitches.

HAPPY HOLIDAYS (70w x 25h)

X	DMC	¼X	B'ST	JPC	COLOR
■	310		╱	8403	black
✳	321	◢	╱	3500	red
S	420			5374	tan
C	666	◢		3046	lt red
◇	783	◢	╱		gold
◉	912	◢	╱	6205	green
•	912		green French Knot		

HAPPY HOLIDAYS (70w x 25h)			
Aida 11	6⅜"	x	2⅜"
Aida 14	5"	x	1⅞"
Aida 18	4"	x	1½"
Hardanger 22	3¼"	x	1¼"

A Frosty Delight

This delicious Date-Nut Ice Cream Topping turns a scoop of plain vanilla ice cream into a rich, frosty delight! The luscious blend of caramel sauce, dates, and pecans can also be used as an extra-special cake topping. For holiday charm, deliver the sauce in a canning jar covered with this papier mâché snowman. When the jar is empty, he'll make a wonderful decoration for a mantel or shelf.

DATE-NUT ICE CREAM TOPPING

- 3 cups granulated sugar
- 2 cans (14 ounces each) sweetened condensed milk
- $\frac{1}{2}$ cup hot water
- 1 box (16 ounces) chopped dates
- 1 cup finely chopped pecans

Combine first 3 ingredients in a large saucepan. Cook over medium heat until sauce thickens (about 5 minutes). Fold in dates and pecans. Store in an airtight container in refrigerator. Give with instructions to reheat.

To reheat, transfer topping to a medium saucepan over low heat. Cook 3 to 5 minutes, stirring constantly, or until heated through. Serve warm over ice cream.

Yield: about $6\frac{1}{2}$ cups topping

SNOWMAN JAR

You will need a 1-pint canning jar; a $4\frac{1}{2}$" x 13" piece of acetate (available at art supply stores); masking tape; aluminum foil; a $2\frac{3}{4}$" dia. plastic foam ball; paring knife; instant papier mâché (we used Celluclay® Instant Papier Mâché); gesso; white, orange, and black acrylic paint; foam brushes; small round paintbrush; 3 approx. $\frac{1}{2}$"w rocks for buttons; 2 approx. $\frac{1}{4}$"w rocks for eyes; 2 approx. 4" long twigs for arms; hot glue gun; glue sticks; matte clear acrylic spray; a $4\frac{1}{2}$" x 22" strip of fabric for scarf; a $3\frac{1}{4}$" dia. black felt hat (available at craft stores); and a $\frac{1}{2}$" dia. VELCRO® brand fastener.

Note: To store topping, remove jar from papier mâché snowman.

1. Overlapping short edges, wrap acetate snugly around side of jar; tape to secure.

2. Leaving top and bottom of acetate tube open, wrap and crush foil pieces around tube, forming a $5\frac{1}{2}$" dia. body shape (Fig. 1). Body shape should be well shaped and firm before papier mâché is added.

Fig. 1

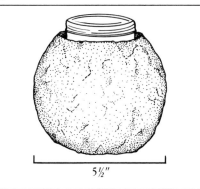

$5\frac{1}{2}$"

3. For head shape, use knife to cut $\frac{1}{4}$" from 1 side of plastic foam ball, forming a flat surface (bottom).

4. Follow Papier Mâché instructions, page 122, to apply papier mâché over foil body shape and head shape. For arms, push end of 1 twig into body at each side. For nose, form a 1" long cone shape with a $\frac{1}{2}$" dia. base from papier mâché. Press base of cone shape onto head; smooth edges onto papier mâché to secure.

5. Apply 1 coat of gesso and 1 coat of white paint to body and head, allowing to dry between coats. Paint nose orange and rocks black; allow to dry.

6. Glue small rocks to head for eyes; glue large rocks to body for buttons. Apply 1 coat of acrylic spray to body and head; allow to dry. Glue hat to head.

7. Paint jar lid white; allow to dry. Glue 1 side of VELCRO® fastener to center top of lid; glue remaining side to center bottom of head.

8. For scarf, fringe short edges of fabric strip $\frac{1}{2}$".

9. Remove jar from body and fill with topping. Replace jar in body and attach head to jar lid. Tie scarf around jar lid.

A new twist on an old favorite, our innovative Peppermint Brittle is a refreshingly different holiday treat. Candy cane pieces are a delicious (and colorful!) addition to the crunchy brittle. Our merry Santa, cleverly crafted from a paper bag and fabric scraps, makes a cheerful carrier for your gift.

PEPPERMINT BRITTLE

    10 6-inch candy canes, broken into
          small pieces
     3 cups granulated sugar
     1 cup light corn syrup
     ½ cup water
     3 tablespoons butter or margarine
     1 teaspoon salt
     2 teaspoons baking soda

Spread candy cane pieces evenly on a large piece of greased aluminum foil.

Grease sides of a large stockpot. Combine next 3 ingredients over medium-low heat, stirring constantly until sugar dissolves. Syrup will become clear. Using a pastry brush dipped in hot water, wash down any sugar crystals on sides of pan. Attach candy thermometer to pan, making sure thermometer does not touch bottom of pan. Increase heat to medium and bring to a boil. Do not stir while syrup is boiling. Continue to cook syrup until it reaches hard crack stage (approximately 300 to 310 degrees) and turns golden brown. Test about ½ teaspoon syrup in ice water. Syrup will form brittle threads in ice water and remain brittle when removed from the water. Remove from heat and add butter and salt; stir until butter melts. Add soda (syrup will foam); stir until soda dissolves. Pour syrup over candy cane pieces. Cool completely on foil. Break into pieces. Store in an airtight container.

Yield: about 2 pounds candy

SANTA BAG

You will need a brown lunch-size paper bag, fabric for hat, artificial lamb fleece for hat trim, muslin for beard, thread to match muslin, 12″ of 3-ply jute, ¾″ dia. shank button with shank removed for nose, black felt-tip pen, 9″ of cotton yarn, a ½″ dia. jingle bell, and craft glue.

1. Trim top of bag straight across.
2. For hat, measure height of bag and divide measurement in half; measure width of front of bag. Cut a piece of fabric the determined measurements. Matching edges, glue fabric piece to top front of bag.
3. For hat trim, cut a 1″w strip of fleece 2″ longer than width of front of bag. Fold each end of strip 1″ to wrong side; glue to secure. Overlapping bottom edge of hat fabric piece ½″, glue trim strip to front of bag.
4. For beard, cut a piece of muslin the same height and 1″ wider than front of bag. Center jute between short edges of muslin. Using a medium width zigzag stitch with a medium stitch length, sew jute along center of muslin. Trim ends of jute even with edges of muslin.
5. Matching short edges, fold muslin in half with jute on inside. At approximately ¾″ intervals, clip ¼″ into short edges of muslin (Fig. 1). At each clip, tear fabric up to zigzag-stitched line.

Fig. 1

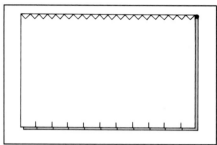

6. Glue folded edge of beard to front of bag. Trim beard to desired length. Glue button to bag for nose. Use pen to draw eyes.
7. Place a plastic bag of candy in bag. To fold top of bag for hat, fold top right corner of bag diagonally to back of bag; fold top left corner of bag straight down to front of bag. Tie cotton yarn into a bow. Glue bow and jingle bell to point of hat. Allow to dry.

"DEER" LITTLE COOKIES

These cute little fellows will delight someone dear to your heart! Our chewy molasses Reindeer Cookies boast pretzel antlers, jelly bean eyes, and a shiny candy "button" nose. You can give them individually for fun treats or present a whole batch in a basket lined with a reversible cloth.

REINDEER COOKIES

½ cup butter or margarine, softened

½ cup firmly packed brown sugar

1 egg

½ cup molasses

3 cups corn flake cereal

1 cup all-purpose flour

½ cup whole wheat flour

½ cup finely chopped pecans

1 teaspoon ground cinnamon

½ teaspoon baking powder

3 dozen large pretzels

3 dozen white jelly beans, cut in half lengthwise

¼ cup semisweet chocolate chips, melted

3 dozen red candy-coated chocolate pieces

In a large bowl, cream butter and sugar until fluffy. Add egg and molasses, beating until smooth. In a blender or a food processor fitted with a steel blade, process next 6 ingredients until mixture resembles a coarse meal. Stir dry ingredients into creamed mixture; knead until a soft dough forms. Divide dough in half. Roll each half into a 2-inch diameter log. Wrap dough in plastic wrap and chill 8 hours or overnight.

Preheat oven to 350 degrees. Cut dough into ¼-inch thick slices. Transfer to a greased baking sheet. Use fingers to pinch each cookie ⅓ from 1 end to resemble reindeer face. Break pretzels into 1½-inch pieces and insert 2 pieces into top of each cookie. Bake 12 to 15 minutes or until golden brown. Cool completely on a wire rack. For eyes, dip 1 end of 2 jelly bean halves in melted chocolate and place on each cookie. For nose, use a small amount of chocolate to secure 1 candy-coated piece to each cookie. Allow chocolate to harden. Store in an airtight container.

Yield: about 3 dozen cookies

For basket liner, cut 2 fabric pieces ½" larger on all sides than desired finished size of liner. Matching right sides and raw edges and leaving an opening for turning, use a ½" seam allowance to sew fabric squares together. Clip corners. Turn right side out; press. Sew final closure by hand.

Spicy Cake Basket

*M*oist and spicy, these little Caramel Apple Cakes are big on holiday flavor! The rich cakes, featuring a combination of apples, walnuts, cinnamon, and maple flavoring, are drizzled with a yummy brown sugar glaze. Our ample recipe makes several small cakes — just right for neighborly gifts. A basket trimmed with spices, greenery, and jute bows makes a nice carrier for one of the cakes; later, it can be used to hold potpourri.

Caramel Apple Cakes

CAKE

- 2 cups granulated sugar
- ½ cup vegetable oil
- 2 eggs
- 1 teaspoon maple-flavored extract
- 2 cups all-purpose flour
- 2 teaspoons baking soda
- 1 teaspoon ground cinnamon
- ½ teaspoon salt
- 3 medium Granny Smith apples, peeled, cored, and coarsely chopped
- 1 cup chopped walnuts

GLAZE

- ¼ cup butter or margarine
- ¼ cup firmly packed brown sugar
- ¼ cup milk
- 1½ cups confectioners sugar, sifted
- ½ teaspoon vanilla extract

Preheat oven to 325 degrees. For cake, mix sugar and oil together in a large bowl. Add eggs and maple extract, beating until smooth. In another large bowl, sift together next 4 ingredients. Add dry ingredients to creamed mixture, mixing well. Fold in apples and walnuts. Spoon batter into 10 greased and floured miniature Bundt cake pans, filling each ½ full. Bake 25 to 30 minutes or until a toothpick inserted in center of cake comes out clean. Turn onto a wire rack to cool completely.

For glaze, melt butter in a medium saucepan over medium heat. Add brown sugar and stir constantly until sugar dissolves. Remove from heat and stir in milk. Beat in confectioners sugar and vanilla using lowest speed of an electric mixer. Drizzle glaze over cakes. Allow glaze to harden. Store in an airtight container.

Yield: ten 4-inch diameter cakes

For basket, hot glue dried bay leaves, preserved boxwood, cinnamon sticks, whole allspice, whole cloves, dried red canella berries, and bows made from 3-ply jute around rim. Place a piece of fabric in basket for liner.

93

SOMETHING FISHY

There's something fishy about this gift basket! It features savory Smoked Salmon Spread and crispy sesame crackers for serving. Designed to delight a fisherman, the basket is wrapped in a "fishnet" and tied with a straw ribbon. The floats are actually red Christmas ornaments that have been dipped in white paint. A catchy tag makes a cute finishing touch.

SMOKED SALMON SPREAD

- 1 package (8 ounces) cream cheese, softened
- 2 teaspoons lime juice
- 6 green onions, finely chopped
- 4 teaspoons finely chopped fresh parsley
- 2 teaspoons ground coriander
- ½ teaspoon ground cayenne pepper
- 10 ounces skinless, boneless smoked salmon

In a large bowl, beat cream cheese and lime juice until fluffy using highest speed of an electric mixer. Add next 4 ingredients; beat until well blended. Stir in salmon. Cover and refrigerate 8 hours or overnight to allow flavors to blend. Serve with crackers or bread. Store in an airtight container in refrigerator.

Yield: about 1½ cups spread

FISHERMAN'S BASKET

You will need a 9″ dia. basket with handle, a cotton net shopping tote, excelsior, green angel hair ribbon, florist wire, 1¾″ dia. red glass ball ornaments, ornament hangers, white acrylic paint, glossy clear acrylic spray, ivory paper, hole punch, red felt-tip pen, cotton string, craft glue, canning jar with lid, and one 4″ square of each of the following: desired fabric, craft batting, and lightweight cardboard.

1. Place basket in tote. Fold top of tote to inside of basket. Fill basket with excelsior.
2. Tie ribbon into a double-loop bow; wire bow to handle.
3. For each float ornament, attach hanger to ornament. Dip bottom half of ornament into paint; hang to dry. Apply 1 coat of acrylic spray to ornament; hang to dry. Hang ornaments on basket.
4. Cut tag shape from paper. Use pen to write "HOOKED ON FISHING" on tag. Punch hole in pointed end of tag. Use string to tie tag to handle.
5. For jar lid insert, follow Steps 1 - 3 of Peppermint Basket instructions, page 70.

ZIPPY LITTLE GIFTS

Our recipe for Green Pepper Jelly makes lots of zippy little gifts for friends from the office or other groups. This versatile condiment is wonderful with chicken or turkey, and it's also delicious with cream cheese and crackers. With their homey hearts, our lids, labels, and tags spruce up the jelly jars. For an embroidered look, draw lines around the hearts to resemble stitches!

GREEN PEPPER JELLY

  5 green peppers
3½ cups granulated sugar
 ½ cup apple cider vinegar
  1 package (3 ounces) liquid pectin
     Green food coloring

Clean peppers; discard seeds and stems. In a blender or food processor fitted with a steel blade, process peppers until puréed. Strain purée, reserving 1 cup juice and 1 cup purée. In a large saucepan, stir together next 2 ingredients and reserved juice and purée. Bring mixture to a boil over high heat, stirring until sugar dissolves. Stir in pectin, bring mixture to a boil again, and boil 1 minute longer. Remove from heat; tint to desired color. Following Sealing Jars instructions, page 120, pour jelly into jars to within ¼ inch of tops. Store in an airtight container in refrigerator. Serve with meat or cream cheese and crackers.

Yield: about 3 half-pints jelly

JELLY JARS

For each jar, you will need tracing paper, craft glue, red permanent felt-tip pen with fine point, desired ribbon, artificial holly sprig (optional), and one 4″ square of each of the following: unbleached muslin fabric, craft batting, lightweight cardboard, desired print fabric, paper-backed fusible web, and cream-colored paper.

1. Cut web slightly smaller than print fabric. Follow manufacturer's instructions to fuse web to wrong side of fabric.
2. Trace heart pattern onto tracing paper; cut out.
3. With web side out, fold print fabric square in half. With straight edge of pattern on fold, center pattern on fabric and draw around pattern. Carefully cut heart from fabric, reserving fabric square. Unfold heart and square.
4. Follow manufacturer's instructions to fuse heart to center of muslin square.

For jar lid insert, follow Steps 1 - 3 of Peppermint Basket instructions, page 70.
5. For label or tag, cut reserved fabric square ⅜″ larger than heart opening. Follow manufacturer's instructions to fuse square to center of paper. For label, cut paper ¼″ larger on all sides than fabric. For tag, cut paper even with fabric.
6. Use pen to draw around hearts; draw lines around edges of hearts to resemble stitches.
7. For jar with label, draw around fabric square and write ''GREEN PEPPER JELLY'' inside heart. Glue label to jar; allow to dry. Tie ribbon into a bow around jar lid.
8. For jar with tag, write name on tag. Knot ribbon around jar lid; thread tag onto 1 ribbon end and tie ends into a bow.
9. If desired, tuck a holly sprig behind bow.

This Christmas Eve, make Santa's stop at your house especially memorable. For his snack, let your child write little pull-out notes to hide inside cupcakes; the messages can be last-minute gift requests, thank-you's, season's greetings, or special news. You can also make a one-of-a-kind frame featuring your child's handwritten letter to display near the snack. By updating the photograph each year, you can show Santa how much your little one has grown!

P.S. The cupcakes are great for school parties, too — classmates will be delighted by the hidden holiday hellos!

MESSAGE TO SANTA CUPCAKES

  1 box (18.25 ounces) chocolate cake mix
  1 can (16 ounces) vanilla-flavored cake frosting

For cupcakes, prepare cake mix according to package directions and bake in foil baking cups. Cool completely on a wire rack. Spread frosting evenly over tops.

For each cupcake, cut three 3-inch lengths of curling ribbon; curl ½ of

each piece. Write desired messages on 1 x 1½-inch pieces of paper. Place 1 message and straight ends of ribbon together. Fold a 2 x 3-inch piece of aluminum foil around message and ribbon ends. Tightly fold foil several more times to securely hold ribbon ends. Repeat for remaining messages. Cut a 1-inch slit in top of each cupcake. Insert 1 foil-wrapped message into each cupcake and smooth icing over. Before eating, pull ribbons to remove message from cupcake. Store in an airtight container.

Yield: about 2 dozen cupcakes

"DEAR SANTA" FRAME

You will need one 8″ x 10″ mat with 4½″ x 6½″ opening and one 5″ x 7″ mat with 3″ x 4½″ opening (we used purchased pre-cut mats), a 10″ square of medium weight cardboard, 22″ of ¹⁄₁₆″ dia. gold cord, a handwritten note to Santa, items to decorate frame (we used miniature toys, packages, and trees; sequins; and glitter-covered paper stars), matte Mod Podge® sealer, high gloss clear epoxy coating (we used Aristocrat™ Epoxy Thick Crystal Clear Coating), tracing paper, 3″ of ½″w ribbon, and spring-type clothespins.

1. (*Note*: Use Mod Podge® sealer for all gluing.) Center 8″ x 10″ mat on 5″ x 7″ mat; glue to secure. Allow to dry.

2. Glue cord along opening of 8″ x 10″ mat. Allow to dry.

3. Tear note to Santa into pieces. Arrange pieces of note and other items on frame until desired effect is achieved; glue to secure. Allow to dry.

4. Allowing to dry between coats, apply 2 coats of sealer to frame front including edges.

5. (*Note:* Read all epoxy coating instructions before beginning.) Carefully

following manufacturer's instructions, apply coating to frame front; allow to dry.

6. Cut an 8″ x 10″ piece from cardboard. Leaving top edges open to insert picture, glue cardboard to back of frame; secure with clothespins. Allow to dry.

7. For easel, trace easel pattern onto tracing paper; cut out. Use pattern and cut 1 piece from cardboard. Fold easel to right side where indicated on pattern by dotted line. With bottom edges even, center wrong side of easel on back of frame; glue area above dotted line to frame. Allow to dry.

8. For easel support, glue 1 end of ribbon on wrong side of easel where indicated by **x** on pattern. Glue remaining end of ribbon to frame back.

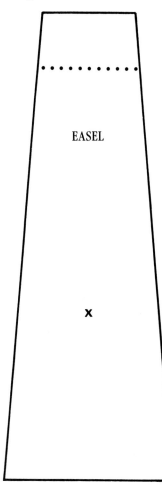

EASEL

x

BASKET OF BUNDLES

A basket of savory Sausage Bundles is a flavorful way to help a friend with her holiday entertaining. Great for snacking or serving as appetizers, the morsels feature a spicy filling neatly wrapped in puff pastry. An edging of prairie points, adapted from an antique quilt border, is sewn from Christmasy fabrics to add a festive touch to the basket liner.

SAUSAGE BUNDLES

   1 package (17¼ ounces) puff
     pastry, thawed
   3 tablespoons Dijon-style mustard
   ¼ cup grated Parmesan cheese
   ½ pound mild pork sausage,
     cooked, crumbled, and
     drained well

Preheat oven to 350 degrees. On a lightly floured surface, use a floured rolling pin to roll out each sheet of pastry to a 10-inch square. Spread mustard evenly over pastry. Sprinkle cheese evenly over mustard. Cut pastry into 2½-inch squares. Press each square into a miniature muffin tin. Spoon about 1 teaspoon sausage into each cup. Bring corners of pastry together and twist to seal. Bake 10 to 12 minutes or until brown. Cool completely on a wire rack. Store in an airtight container in refrigerator. Give with instructions for reheating.

To reheat, preheat oven to 300 degrees. Bake uncovered on an ungreased baking sheet 3 to 5 minutes or until heated through.

Yield: about 2½ dozen sausage bundles

BASKET LINER

For an 18¾" square basket liner, you will need two 17½" fabric squares, thread to match fabric squares, and fabric scraps for prairie point edging.

1. For edging, cut a 3¼" square from a fabric scrap. With wrong sides together, fold square in half diagonally. Fold in half again, forming a small triangle (Fig. 1); press. Repeat to make 36 triangles.

Fig. 1

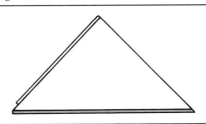

2. (*Note:* Adjust overlap of triangles if necessary to fit edges of liner.) Matching right sides and raw edges and overlapping triangles approximately 1¾", refer to Fig. 2 to baste 9 triangles to each edge of 1 liner fabric square.

Fig. 2

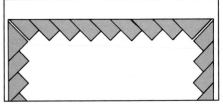

3. Matching right sides and raw edges, place liner fabric squares together. Leaving an opening for turning, use a ½" seam allowance to sew squares together. Cut corners diagonally and trim seam allowance. Turn liner right side out; press. Sew final closure by hand. Remove any visible basting threads.

SANTA COOKIE TREE

*O*ur adorable Santa Cookies make fun, edible ornaments. They're really easy to make by decorating purchased peanut-shaped cookies with icing, candied cherries, and raisins. Whether presented on a miniature tree or tucked in a holiday basket, the jolly cookies will delight friends of all ages.

SANTA COOKIES

1 package (16 ounces) peanut-
    shaped peanut butter
    sandwich cookies
  Purchased red and white
    decorating icing
  Red candied cherries
  Raisins

For each cookie, use a large star tip to pipe red icing on cookie to resemble stocking cap. Use a large star tip to pipe white icing on cookie to resemble beard, mustache, and trim on cap. For nose, secure a small piece of candied cherry on cookie with icing. For eyes, secure small pieces of raisins on cookie with icing. Allow icing to harden. Store in an airtight container.

Yield: about 2½ dozen cookies

To hang each cookie from tree, insert an ornament hanger into cookie filling. Remove hanger before eating cookie.

SIMPLY DIVINE GIFTS

Gaily decorated Shaker boxes make great gifts by themselves, but when they're filled with homemade treats, they're twice as nice! For a divine way of telling friends "You're extra special," tuck squares of light, fluffy Cherry Divinity into the personalized boxes.

CHERRY DIVINITY

2 cups granulated sugar
½ cup light corn syrup
½ cup water
⅛ teaspoon salt
2 egg whites
1 teaspoon vanilla extract
1 cup chopped red candied cherries
½ cup finely chopped walnuts

Grease sides of a large stockpot. Combine first 4 ingredients in stockpot over medium-low heat, stirring constantly until sugar dissolves. Syrup will become clear. Using a pastry brush dipped in hot water, wash down any sugar crystals on sides of stockpot. Attach candy thermometer to stockpot, making sure thermometer does not touch bottom of stockpot. Increase heat to medium and bring to a boil. Do not stir while syrup is boiling.

When syrup reaches approximately 240 degrees, beat egg whites in a large bowl until stiff using highest speed of an electric mixer; set aside.

Continue to cook syrup until it reaches firm-ball stage (approximately 242 to 248 degrees). Test about ½ teaspoon syrup in ice water. Syrup will form a firm ball in ice water but flatten if pressed when removed from the water. While beating egg whites at low speed, slowly pour syrup into egg whites. Add vanilla and increase speed of mixer to high. Continue to beat until candy is no longer glossy and a stationary column forms when beaters are lifted. Fold in cherries and walnuts. Pour into a greased 8-inch square baking dish. Allow to harden. Cut into 1-inch squares. Store in an airtight container.

Yield: about 5 dozen squares divinity

SMALL GIFT BOXES

For each ribbon-tied box, you will need 2 print fabrics and desired ribbon.
For each Santa box, you will need white cotton-blend fabric, print fabric or ribbon to cover side of lid, ribbon for bow (optional), tracing paper, graphite transfer paper, black permanent felt-tip pen with fine point, and red, dk red, peach, green, and pink watercolor markers.
You will also need a 4" or 5" dia. Shaker box, fabric marking pencil, craft batting, and craft glue.

1. (*Note:* Allow to dry after each glue step.) For ribbon-tied box, place lid on wrong side of print fabric; draw around lid with fabric marking pencil. Cut out fabric ½" outside drawn line. Clip fabric at ½" intervals to within ⅛" of line.
2. Use lid as a pattern and cut 1 circle from batting; glue batting to lid. Center fabric circle right side up on batting. Glue clipped edges of fabric to side of lid.
3. Cut a strip of fabric 1" wider than side of lid and 2" longer than circumference of lid. Press edges ½" to wrong side. Glue strip to side of lid.
4. Place divinity in box. Tie ribbon into a bow around box.
5. For Santa box, trace desired portions of pattern onto tracing paper. Use transfer paper to transfer design to white fabric. Use pens to color design and to write desired message around design.
6. Follow Steps 1 and 2 to cover lid with fabric Santa.
7. (*Note:* Follow Step 3 or Step 7 to cover side of lid.) Cut a length of ribbon the same width as side of lid 1" longer than circumference of lid. Glue ribbon to side of lid.
8. Place divinity in box. If desired, tie a length of ribbon into a bow; glue to top of box.

TUXEDO GREETINGS

The tag reads: *Should auld acquaintance be forgot— and never brought to mind? HAPPY NEW YEAR*

To wish a favorite gentleman "Happy New Year" or "Merry Christmas," present a batch of Irish Cream Fudge in a charming tuxedo box. Walnuts and Irish Cream liqueur lend distinctive flavor to this rich, creamy candy. With our clear instructions, you can easily turn an ordinary shirt box into a handsome carrier for your Yuletide offering. He'll love this stylish holiday remembrance!

IRISH CREAM FUDGE

1 cup finely chopped walnuts
4 cups granulated sugar
1 cup evaporated milk
⅓ cup light corn syrup
6 tablespoons butter or margarine
2 tablespoons honey
½ teaspoon salt
½ cup Irish Cream liqueur
1½ cups (9 ounces) semisweet chocolate chips, melted

Spread nuts evenly in bottom of a greased 8 x 11-inch baking dish. Grease sides of a large stockpot. Combine next 6 ingredients in stockpot and cook over medium-low heat, stirring constantly until sugar dissolves. Using a pastry brush dipped in hot water, wash down any sugar crystals on sides of pan. Attach candy thermometer to pan, making sure thermometer does not touch bottom of pan. Increase heat to medium and bring to a boil. Do not stir while syrup is boiling. Cook until syrup reaches soft ball stage (approximately 234 to 240 degrees). Test about ½ teaspoon syrup in ice water. Syrup should easily form a ball in ice water but flatten when held in your hand. Place stockpot in 2 inches of cold water in sink. Add liqueur to syrup; do not stir until syrup cools to approximately 110 degrees. Add chocolate and beat fudge using medium speed of an electric mixer until it is no longer glossy and thickens. Pour over nuts. Allow to cool completely. Cut into 1-inch squares. Store in an airtight container in refrigerator.

Yield: about 7 dozen squares fudge

TUXEDO GIFT BOX

You will need an 8½" x 11½" x 1½" shirt box, ¼ yd of 44"w plaid taffeta fabric, three ⁵⁄₁₆" dia. shank buttons with shanks removed, white paper, craft glue, tracing paper, and transparent tape.

1. Follow Gift Box 1 instructions, page 123, to cover box with white paper.
2. For shirt pleats, cut 4 strips from white paper 11½" long and the following widths: 2½", 3⅛", 3¾", and 4⅜". Fold long edges of each strip ½" to 1 side (wrong side). Layer strips from widest to narrowest; glue to secure. Center and glue pleats to top of box.
3. For collar, use pattern and follow Transferring Patterns, page 122. Use pattern and cut 1 collar from white paper. Fold collar to 1 side (right side) along fold lines (indicated by dotted lines on pattern). Center collar along top edge of top of lid; glue to secure.
4. For tie, cut a 3⅝" x 24" strip from fabric. Press long edges 1" to wrong side. Cut strip into one 11", one 10", and one 3" strip. Overlap ends of 11" strip 1" to form a loop; glue to secure. Repeat for 10" strip. With overlapped areas at center back, stack loops together. Wrap 3" strip around centers of loops; glue ends at back to secure. Glue tie to lid.
5. For cummerbund, cut one 2½" x 10½" strip and four 2" x 13½" strips from fabric. Press 1 long edge of 2½" wide strip ½" to wrong side. Press both long edges of the remaining strips ½" to wrong side.
6. Referring to Fig. 1, center pressed edge of 2½" wide strip along bottom edge of bottom side of lid; glue to secure. Glue ends of strip to sides of lid. Glue remaining edge to top of lid.

Fig. 1

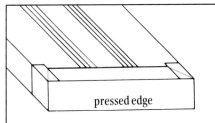

pressed edge

7. Center 1 long pressed edge of one 2" wide strip along bottom edge of top of lid; wrap strip around box lid, gluing ends of strip to inside of lid. Overlapping first 2" wide strip ½", repeat to glue a second strip to lid. Repeat to attach remaining strips.
8. Glue buttons to lid.

CREATE-A-COOKIE KIT

*I*maginative youngsters will find everything they need to make holiday cookies in this cute Create-A-Cookie Kit. Using our recipes, you make the edible paint and the dough for the White Chocolate Cookies and pack them in the whimsical paint pail along with instructions for making the cookies. To complete the kit, add cookie cutters, brushes, and a painter's drop cloth. After the children cut out and paint the dough shapes, the cookies are ready to bake and enjoy!

WHITE CHOCOLATE COOKIES

COOKIE DOUGH

   1 cup butter or margarine, softened
1½ cups granulated sugar
   2 eggs
   1 teaspoon vanilla extract
2½ cups white chocolate pieces, melted
   5 cups all-purpose flour
   1 teaspoon baking soda
   1 teaspoon salt

EDIBLE ''TEMPERA'' PAINTS

   3 egg yolks
     Green, red, and blue food coloring

For dough, cream butter and sugar in a large bowl until fluffy. Add eggs and vanilla, beating until smooth. Stir in chocolate. In another large bowl, sift together next 3 ingredients. Stir dry ingredients into creamed mixture; knead until a soft dough forms. Place dough in a resealable plastic bag and refrigerate.

For paints, drop each yolk into a separate bowl. Stir each yolk with a fork until smooth. For green, add ¼ teaspoon green food coloring; mix well. For red, add ½ teaspoon red food coloring; mix well. For black, add 1¼ teaspoons green, 1½ teaspoons red, and 5 drops blue food coloring; mix well. Place each color paint in a small jar with lid and refrigerate. Give with instructions for making cookies.

To make cookies, preheat oven to 350 degrees. On a lightly floured surface, use a floured rolling pin to roll out dough to ¼-inch thickness. Use cookie cutters to cut out dough. Transfer to a greased baking sheet. Use a paintbrush to paint cookies as desired. Bake 10 to 12 minutes or until light brown. Cool completely on a wire rack. Store in an airtight container.

Yield: about 4 dozen 3-inch cookies

PAINT PAIL

You will need a metal pail (we found our 2-quart pail at a paint store), gesso, desired color acrylic paint, foam brushes, small round paintbrush, and glossy clear acrylic spray.

1. Apply 2 coats of gesso to entire pail, allowing to dry between coats.
2. Paint inside of pail desired color; using same color, paint outside of pail to resemble dripping paint. Allow to dry.
3. Apply 1 coat of acrylic spray to pail. Allow to dry.

Mini Gifts

There's a refreshing surprise inside these brownies: a layer of chocolate mint candy is baked in the center! Quick and easy to prepare, they make great mini gifts for classmates and coworkers during the holidays. You can personalize each little gift by using our painted Santa clothespins to attach holly-shaped name tags to the packages. Later, the clips will make cheerful ornaments for the Christmas tree.

MINT LAYERED BROWNIES

- ½ cup butter or margarine
- 2 ounces unsweetened chocolate
- 1 cup granulated sugar
- 1 teaspoon vanilla extract
- 2 eggs
- ¾ cup all-purpose flour
- ½ teaspoon baking soda
- ¼ teaspoon salt
- 1 dozen 1½-inch diameter chocolate-covered mint candies

Preheat oven to 350 degrees. In a medium saucepan, melt butter and chocolate over low heat. Remove from heat; transfer to a large bowl. Add sugar and vanilla; beat until well blended. Add eggs 1 at a time, beating well after each addition. In a medium bowl, sift together next 3 ingredients. Add dry ingredients to chocolate mixture; stir until well blended. Pour ½ of batter into a greased 8-inch square baking pan. Place mint candies evenly on batter. Top with remaining batter. Bake 30 to 35 minutes or until set in center. Cool completely in pan. Cut into 1½-inch squares. Store in an airtight container.

Yield: about 2 dozen brownies

SANTA CLOTHESPINS

For each clothespin, you will need a wooden spring-type clothespin; white, red, peach, pink, dk pink, and black acrylic paint; small round paintbrush; liner paintbrush; and matte clear acrylic spray.

1. (*Note:* Allow to dry after each paint color.) Paint clothespin red.
2. For face, paint a ¼" wide band of peach ¼" from top on 1 side of clothespin. Use pink to paint cheeks on bottom half of peach band. Use white to paint hat trim, beard, and mustache. Use dk pink to paint a dot for nose and a dot for mouth. Use liner brush and black to paint eyes. Use liner brush and white to paint highlights in eyes.
3. Spray clothespin with acrylic spray; allow to dry.

CHRISTMAS ELEGANCE

*F*or a Christmas gift with the elegance of yesteryear, offer these lacy Cream-Filled Fruitcake Cones on our handsome serving plate. The crispy cones feature colorful bits of candied pineapple and a sweet filling of brandy-flavored whipped cream. The decorative dish, which resembles antique cranberry glass, is easy to make by adorning a clear glass plate with pretty cutouts and ruby paint.

CREAM-FILLED FRUITCAKE CONES

COOKIES

- ⅔ cup light corn syrup
- ½ cup plus 2 tablespoons butter or margarine, softened
- ¼ cup firmly packed brown sugar
- 1¼ teaspoons ground ginger
- ⅛ teaspoon salt
- 1 cup all-purpose flour
- 2 tablespoons brandy
- 1 package (4 ounces) candied pineapple (assorted colors), minced

FILLING

- 1 cup whipping cream
- 1 tablespoon granulated sugar
- 1 teaspoon vanilla extract
- ½ teaspoon ground cinnamon
- 2 teaspoons brandy

For cookies, preheat oven to 350 degrees. In a large saucepan, combine first 5 ingredients. Bring to a boil over medium heat, stirring constantly. Remove from heat; whisk in flour and brandy. Stir in pineapple. Set pan in 2 inches of hot water to keep batter warm. Drop teaspoonfuls of batter approximately 4 inches apart on a greased baking sheet. Bake 8 to 10 minutes or until golden brown. Cool on pan 30 seconds; remove and quickly shape cookies around the handle of a wooden spoon to form a cone. Place cookies seam side down on a wire rack to cool completely. When cool, remove spoon.

For filling, whip cream in a chilled large bowl until foamy. Add next 3 ingredients; continue to beat until stiff. Fold in brandy. Using a pastry tube fitted with a large star tip, pipe filling into cookies. Store in an airtight container in refrigerator.

Yield: about 7 dozen cookies

DECOUPAGE PLATE

You will need a clear glass plate, motifs cut from gold paper doilies and wrapping paper, ⁵⁄₁₆"w gold braid trim, matte Mod Podge® sealer, foam brush, and burgundy Floralife® Perfect Touch Color Collection® floral spray (available at florist shops).

Note: Plate is for decorative use. Wipe clean with a damp cloth.

1. Use sealer to glue right sides of motifs to back of plate; glue braid ¼" from edge on back of plate. Allow to dry.
2. Apply 2 coats of sealer to back of plate, allowing to dry between coats.
3. Spray back of plate evenly with 2 light coats of floral spray, allowing to dry between coats.
4. Repeat Step 2.

A Stellar Gift

*S*wirls of rich chocolate and vanilla make Marble Fudge an extra-special gift. For a shining presentation, package the candy in our pretty box — the star-shaped cutout provides a stellar view of the delicious delights inside!

Marble Fudge

- 2 cups granulated sugar
- 1 cup whipping cream
- ½ cup butter or margarine
- 1 tablespoon light corn syrup
- 1 teaspoon vanilla extract
- ½ cup (3 ounces) semisweet chocolate chips, melted

Grease sides of a large stockpot. Combine first 4 ingredients in stockpot and cook over medium-low heat, stirring constantly until sugar dissolves. Using a pastry brush dipped in hot water, wash down any sugar crystals on sides of stockpot. Attach candy thermometer to pan, making sure thermometer does not touch bottom of stockpot. Increase heat to medium and bring to a boil. Do not stir while syrup is boiling. Cook until syrup reaches soft ball stage (approximately 234 to 240 degrees). Test about ½ teaspoon syrup in ice water. Syrup should easily form a ball in ice water but flatten when held in your hand. Place stockpot in 2 inches of cold water in sink. Add vanilla; do not stir until syrup cools to approximately 110 degrees. Remove from water. Using medium speed of an electric mixer, beat fudge until it thickens and is no longer glossy. Pour

into a greased 8-inch square baking pan. Drizzle chocolate on top of fudge. Using tip of a knife, gently swirl chocolate into fudge. Cool until firm. Cut into 1-inch squares. Store in airtight container in refrigerator.

Yield: about 5 dozen squares fudge

Star Box

You will need a cardboard box with lid (lid must be at least 9″ square to accommodate star pattern), tracing paper, craft knife, cutting mat or a thick layer of newspapers, wrapping paper, transparent tape, craft glue, a 9″ square of clear cellophane, gold gummed stars (optional), desired cord and ribbon, and waxed paper to line box.

1. Use star pattern and follow Transferring Patterns, page 122.
2. Center star pattern on box lid; draw around pattern. Cut star shape from lid.
3. Follow Gift Box 1 instructions, page 123, to cover box (cover star-shaped opening). Place lid top side down on cutting mat. Cutting ½″ inside edge of star shape, use craft knife to cut star shape from wrapping paper. At each corner of star, clip edges of paper to within 1/16″ of edges of cardboard. Fold cut edges of wrapping paper to inside of lid; glue to secure.
4. Center and glue cellophane square inside lid.
5. If desired, decorate box with gummed stars.
6. Line box with waxed paper; place fudge in box. Place lid on box; tie ribbon and cord into a bow around box.

ANGELS OF GOLD

These heavenly creations will make an elegant Christmas surprise for someone special. Shaped in an angel cookie mold, the Gilded Nutmeg Cookies are embellished with gold petal dust, an edible decorative powder available at gourmet food stores. Your friend is sure to agree that these rich, radiant treats are out of this world!

GILDED NUTMEG COOKIES

½ cup butter or margarine, softened
1 cup firmly packed brown sugar
½ cup granulated sugar
1 egg
1 teaspoon vanilla extract
2 cups all-purpose flour
1 teaspoon ground nutmeg
¼ teaspoon salt
  Gold petal dust (available at gourmet food stores)
  Vodka (optional)

Preheat oven to 350 degrees. In a large bowl, cream butter and sugars until fluffy. Add egg and vanilla; beat until smooth. In a medium bowl, sift together next 3 ingredients. Add to creamed mixture; knead until a soft dough forms. Press dough into a greased cookie mold, filling it evenly to top. Use a sharp knife to loosen edges of dough. Invert mold onto a greased baking sheet. Tap lightly to release dough. Repeat for remaining dough.

Bake 10 to 12 minutes or until edges of cookies are brown. Transfer to a wire rack to cool completely.

To decorate cookies, use a small round paintbrush to brush petal dust onto cookies. If desired, mix petal dust with a few drops of vodka to form a thin paste and brush onto cookies; allow to dry. Store in an airtight container.

Yield: about seven 6½-inch cookies

PRETTY AND PINK

*P*retty and pink, Cranberry Liqueur is a delightful way to say "Happy Holidays"! The creamy beverage has a tart, tangy taste enhanced with a hint of cinnamon. For an attractive presentation, include a set of glasses that you've etched with a holly motif.

CRANBERRY LIQUEUR

- 1 can (14 ounces) sweetened condensed milk
- 2 cups vodka
- 1 can (16 ounces) jellied cranberry sauce
- 1 can (12 ounces) frozen cranberry-orange juice cocktail, thawed
- 1 cup half and half
- 1 teaspoon ground cinnamon

Combine all ingredients in a blender and blend until smooth. Cover and chill overnight to allow flavors to blend. Store in an airtight container in refrigerator.

Yield: about 8 cups liqueur

ETCHED LIQUEUR GLASSES

For each glass, you will need a liqueur glass, a 2″ square of white self-adhesive plastic (Con-tact® paper), graphite transfer paper, tracing paper, masking tape, craft knife, a paper towel, foam brush, glass etching cream (available at craft stores), and rubber gloves.

1. Trace holly pattern onto tracing paper.
2. Use transfer paper to transfer pattern onto plastic side of self-adhesive plastic.
3. Remove backing from plastic and place plastic on glass, smoothing out bubbles and wrinkles. Cover edges of plastic with masking tape.
4. Use craft knife to cut out design. Gently clean cutout areas on glass with paper towel.
5. (*Note:* Wear rubber gloves to protect hands while using etching cream.) Follow manufacturer's instructions to apply etching cream to design. After 2 minutes, remove cream under running water.
6. Remove tape and plastic from glass. Wash glass before using.

Given to your favorite cook or hostess, a basket of Sugarplum Tarts and our gingerbread doll apron will deliver lots of Yuletide cheer. The flaky tarts, with their creamy plum filling, are sure to become a Christmas tradition. And the adorable cross-stitched apron will bring inspiration to your friend's holiday baking for many years to come.

SUGARPLUM TARTS

CRUST

- $\frac{3}{4}$ cup butter or margarine, softened
- $\frac{1}{2}$ cup granulated sugar
- 2 egg yolks
- 1$\frac{3}{4}$ cups all-purpose flour
- $\frac{1}{8}$ teaspoon salt
- $\frac{3}{4}$ teaspoon vanilla extract

FILLING

- 1 jar (10 ounces) red plum jam
- 1 cup granulated sugar
- $\frac{1}{4}$ cup all-purpose flour
- $\frac{1}{8}$ teaspoon salt
- 1 cup whipping cream
- $\frac{1}{2}$ cup half and half
- 2 teaspoons vanilla extract

Preheat oven to 350 degrees. For crust, cream butter and sugar in a large bowl until fluffy. Add egg yolks 1 at a time, beating well after each addition. Add remaining ingredients; stir until a soft dough forms. Press about 1$\frac{1}{2}$ teaspoons dough into bottoms and up sides of greased miniature muffin tins.

For filling, spoon about $\frac{1}{2}$ teaspoon jam into bottom of each crust; set aside. In a large bowl, sift together next 3 ingredients. Add remaining ingredients. Using highest speed of an electric mixer, beat cream mixture until thick and fluffy, about 4 to 5 minutes. Spoon about 1 tablespoon cream mixture into each crust. Bake 30 to 35 minutes or until filling is set in center and crust is brown. Cool in pan 10 minutes. Transfer to a wire rack to cool completely. Store in an airtight container in refrigerator.

Yield: about 5 dozen tarts

HOLIDAY APRON

You will need a natural Janlynn® Personal-Wares® apron with Ivory Aida (14 ct) insert, embroidery floss (see color key), 16" of $\frac{1}{4}$"w red satin ribbon, thread to match ribbon, and two $\frac{5}{8}$" dia. jingle bells.

1. Work design on apron insert using 2 strands of floss for Cross Stitch and 1 for Backstitch.
2. Tack 1 jingle bell to apron at each side of stitched design.
3. Cut ribbon in half. Tie each length into a bow; trim ends. Tack 1 bow above each bell.

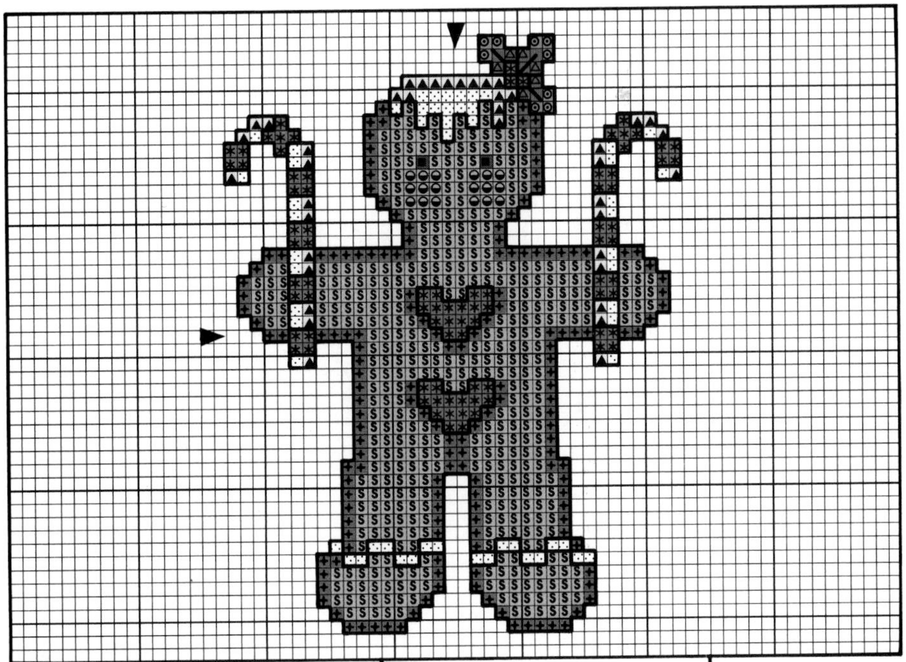

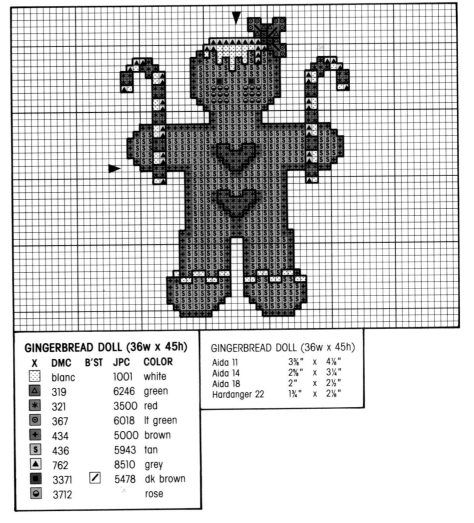

GINGERBREAD DOLL (36w x 45h)

X	DMC	B'ST	JPC	COLOR
⋯	blanc		1001	white
△	319		6246	green
✱	321		3500	red
⊙	367		6018	lt green
+	434		5000	brown
S	436		5943	tan
▲	762		8510	grey
■	3371	⁄	5478	dk brown
◒	3712			rose

GINGERBREAD DOLL (36w x 45h)

Aida 11	3$\frac{3}{8}$"	x	4$\frac{1}{8}$"
Aida 14	2$\frac{5}{8}$"	x	3$\frac{1}{4}$"
Aida 18	2"	x	2$\frac{1}{2}$"
Hardanger 22	1$\frac{3}{4}$"	x	2$\frac{1}{8}$"

REINDEER DELIVERY

Yummy Chocolate Peanut Butter is the ultimate combination of two favorite flavors! Great on cookies, the creamy spread will be irresistible to grownups and children alike. Prancing wooden reindeer cutouts and a bright cloth make an ordinary basket a cute (and inexpensive!) way to deliver your gift.

CHOCOLATE PEANUT BUTTER

- 1½ cups smooth peanut butter
- ½ cup semisweet chocolate chips, melted
- ¼ cup butter or margarine, softened
- ¼ cup confectioners sugar
- 1 teaspoon vanilla extract
- 1 teaspoon instant coffee granules
- 1 teaspoon hot water

In a large bowl, combine first 5 ingredients; stir until smooth. Combine coffee granules and water; stir until coffee dissolves. Stir coffee into peanut butter mixture. Serve with cookies or crackers. Store in an airtight container.

Yield: about 2 cups peanut butter

For basket, hot glue purchased 2″ wide wooden reindeer cutouts around basket rim. Line basket with a fabric square.

CRUNCHY MUNCHIES

The rich flavor of hollandaise gives this snack mix a buttery taste. A crunchy combination of peanuts, crackers, and pretzels, the mix is sure to be a favorite for holiday munching. To surprise a favorite snacker, pack the mix in a pretty jar or tin and deliver it in a homey gift bag.

HOLLANDAISE SNACK MIX

- ½ cup butter
- 2 packages (0.9 ounces each) hollandaise sauce mix
- 1 tablespoon Worcestershire sauce
- 2 teaspoons garlic powder
- 2 cups unsalted dry-roasted peanuts
- 2 cups Ritz Bits™ crackers
- 2 cups stick pretzels

Preheat oven to 300 degrees. In a small saucepan, melt butter over medium heat. Stir in next 3 ingredients. In a large bowl, mix together peanuts, crackers, and pretzels. Pour butter mixture over peanut mixture. Toss until well coated. Spread evenly on a baking sheet. Bake 15 to 20 minutes, stirring occasionally. Transfer to paper towels to cool completely. Store in an airtight container.

Yield: about 6 cups snack mix

*Smooth and creamy
Cheese Bisque will receive a
warm welcome from a
friend on a chilly December
day. A wonderful
combination of cheese,
vegetables, and spices, this
soup has a mellow flavor
that's sure to please. Hand-
painted in bright holiday
colors, a wooden basket
with a fabric liner is a
cheerful way to deliver your
gift. After the soup is gone,
your friend will find many
uses for the little crate.*

CHEESE BISQUE

- 2 cups water
- 3 medium carrots, peeled and finely chopped
- 6 stalks celery, finely chopped
- 6 green onions, finely chopped
- ½ cup butter or margarine
- 1 large onion, finely chopped
- 1 cup all-purpose flour
- 3 cans (10½ ounces each) chicken broth
- 2 cups milk
- 3 packages (6 ounces each) Kraft® process cheese food with garlic, cut into pieces
- 2 teaspoons salt
- 1 teaspoon ground white pepper
- ½ teaspoon cayenne pepper

In a large stockpot, bring water to a boil over high heat. Add next 3 ingredients, reduce heat to medium, and simmer 5 minutes. In a small saucepan, melt butter over medium heat. Add onion; sauté until brown. Stir in flour. Add flour mixture to vegetable mixture; stir until well blended. Add chicken broth and milk; whisk until well blended. Add remaining ingredients, stirring constantly until cheese melts and bisque is smooth. Bring to a boil; remove from heat. Store in an airtight container in refrigerator. Give with instructions for reheating.

To reheat, transfer bisque to a large stockpot. Cook over medium heat, stirring occasionally, until heated through.

Yield: about 12 to 14 servings

BOW BASKET

You will need a wooden basket with bow shapes cut into sides (we found our basket at a craft store; any basket with an area suitable for painting may be used); tracing paper; graphite transfer paper; white, red, green, dk green, grey, and black acrylic paint; foam brush; paintbrushes; matte clear acrylic spray; and a fabric square to line basket.

1. (*Note*: Allow to dry between each color or coat of paint.) Paint entire basket red; paint outside of handle white.
2. Trace bow pattern onto tracing paper. With bow centered under basket handle, use transfer paper to transfer bow to each side of basket, extending ribbon to bottom edge of basket. Extend ribbon to top edge of basket if necessary.
3. For 1 side of basket, paint bow and ribbon white. Paint holly leaves green. Use dk green to shade ½ of each leaf. Use grey to shade handle, bow, and ribbon. Use black to add detail lines to bow, ribbon, and holly leaves. Repeat for remaining side of basket.
4. Apply 2 coats of acrylic spray to basket, allowing to dry between coats.
5. Line basket with fabric square.

A BASKET OF JOY

Share the joy of the season with this pretty holiday basket. The fruity Peach Tea Mix, packed in a plaid fabric bag, is a quick way to enjoy a cup of steaming, aromatic tea. For a lasting reminder of your gift, include our cross-stitched "Joy" ornament featuring a classic snowflake design. A mug for the tea is a thoughtful finishing touch, and don't forget the serving instructions!

JOY ORNAMENT

You will need two 6″ squares of Blueberry Aida (18 ct), white embroidery floss and floss for twisted cord hanger (we used DMC 931), and polyester fiberfill.

1. Leaving grey area of chart unstitched, work design on 1 fabric square using 2 strands of floss for Cross Stitch and 1 for Backstitch.
2. Place fabric squares wrong sides together. Stitching through both layers of fabric, work 3 sides of border (grey area of chart). Stuff ornament lightly with fiberfill; work remaining side of border.
3. Trim ornament 9 fabric threads from border. Remove fabric threads to within ⅛″ of border.
4. For twisted cord hanger, cut four 18″ lengths from floss. Place lengths together. Knot lengths together 1″ from 1 end; repeat for remaining end. Fasten 1 end to a stationary object. Pull floss taut and twist tightly. Matching knotted ends, fold floss in half and allow to twist together; knot ends together to secure. Pull cord through fingers to evenly distribute twists. Tack ends of cord to top corners on back of ornament.

PEACH TEA MIX

  1 cup instant tea mix
  1 box (3 ounces) peach-flavored gelatin
  2 cups granulated sugar

Combine all ingredients in a large bowl; mix well. Store in an airtight container. Give with instructions to serve.

To serve, stir about 2 teaspoons tea mix into 8 ounces hot water.

Yield: about 3½ cups tea mix

For fabric bag, cut a 7″ x 23″ piece of fabric and follow Steps 2 - 4 of Fabric Bag instructions, page 123. Place a plastic bag of tea mix in bag. Tie two 18″ lengths of ribbon in a bow around bag.

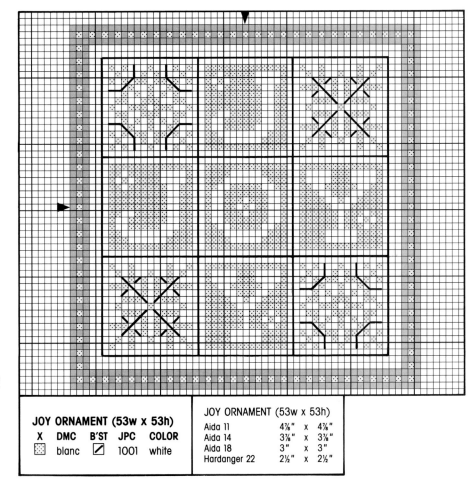

JOY ORNAMENT (53w x 53h)			
X	DMC	B'ST	JPC	COLOR
▨	blanc	✓	1001	white

JOY ORNAMENT (53w x 53h)		
Aida 11	4⅞″	x	4⅞″
Aida 14	3⅞″	x	3⅞″
Aida 18	3″	x	3″
Hardanger 22	2½″	x	2½″

JINGLE ALL THE WAY

This delectable Pecan-Raisin Wreath is ideal to take to a holiday hostess! Easy to make with frozen yeast rolls, the bread is enhanced by pecans, raisins, and cinnamon. A simple basket makes a convenient carrier. Shiny bells attached to the basket liner will jingle all the way to your friend's house!

PECAN-RAISIN WREATH

- ½ cup butter or margarine, divided
- ½ cup firmly packed brown sugar
- 1 tablespoon corn syrup
- 18 pecan halves
- ⅓ cup chopped pecans
- ⅓ cup raisins
- 3 tablespoons granulated sugar
- ¼ teaspoon ground cinnamon
- 10 frozen uncooked white dinner rolls, thawed

Preheat oven to 350 degrees. In a small saucepan, combine ¼ cup butter, brown sugar, and corn syrup over medium heat. Cook, stirring constantly, until sugar dissolves. Pour sugar mixture into a greased 8-inch ring mold. Place pecan halves upside down on sugar mixture.

Melt remaining butter in a small saucepan. In a small bowl, stir together chopped pecans, raisins, granulated sugar, and cinnamon. Dip each roll into melted butter and place in nut mixture. Spoon nut mixture over, covering each roll completely. Arrange rolls with sides touching in mold. Sprinkle remaining nut mixture over tops of rolls. Bake

35 to 40 minutes or until golden brown. Cool in pan 15 minutes. Turn onto a wire rack to cool completely. Store in an airtight container. Give with instructions for serving.

Bread may be served warm or at room temperature. To reheat, preheat oven to 350 degrees. Bake uncovered on an ungreased baking sheet 3 to 5 minutes or until heated through.

Yield: about 10 servings

JINGLE BELL BASKET

You will need a basket with handle, two fabrics for liner, 1 yd of ¹⁄₁₆"w satin ribbon, thread to match fabrics and ribbon, four ½" dia. jingle bells, matte clear acrylic spray, and black permanent felt-tip pen with fine point.

1. Apply 2 coats of acrylic spray to basket, allowing to dry between coats.
2. Use pen to write "Jingle Bells, Jingle Bells, Jingle All the Way" on basket handle.
3. For liner, follow basket liner instructions, page 92.
4. Sew 1 jingle bell to each corner of liner. Cut four 9" lengths from ribbon. Tie each length into a bow; trim ends. Tack 1 bow above each jingle bell.

ELEGANT BROWNIE BAG

*R*aspberry Fudge Brownies make irresistible Christmas treats! Walnuts and raspberry jam add delicious flavor to the moist brownies. For those occasions when you don't have time to craft a container for your gift, take advantage of the wonderful array of gift bags available in stores. An assortment of colors and styles makes it easy to coordinate them with your gift. We chose an elegant bag, liner, and bow to reflect the richness of our brownies.

RASPBERRY FUDGE BROWNIES

- ½ cup butter or margarine, softened
- 1 cup granulated sugar
- 3 eggs
- 1 jar (12 ounces) raspberry jam, divided
- 18 2-inch diameter chocolate wafer cookies, finely ground
- ½ cup all-purpose flour
- 1 cup (6 ounces) semisweet chocolate chips
- 1 cup chopped walnuts

Preheat oven to 350 degrees. In a large bowl, cream butter and sugar until fluffy. Add eggs and ½ cup jam, beating until smooth. Add ground cookies and flour; mix well. Pour batter into a greased 8 x 11-inch baking dish. Sprinkle chocolate chips evenly over batter. Bake 35 to 40 minutes or until a toothpick inserted in center comes out clean. In a small saucepan, melt remaining jam over low heat, stirring constantly. Stir in walnuts. Pour jam mixture over brownies. Cool completely in pan. Cut into 2-inch squares. Store in an airtight container.

Yield: about 1½ dozen brownies

KITCHEN TIPS

MEASURING INGREDIENTS

Liquid measuring cups have a rim above the measuring line to keep liquid ingredients from spilling. Nested measuring cups (¼, ⅓, ½, and 1 cup) are used to measure dry ingredients, butter, and shortening. Measuring spoons (⅛, ¼, ½, 1 teaspoon, and 1 tablespoon) are used for measuring both dry and liquid ingredients.

To measure flour or granulated sugar: Dip nested measuring cup into ingredient and level top of cup with knife. Do not pack down with spoon.

To measure brown sugar: Pack into nested measuring cup and level top of cup with knife. Sugar should hold its shape when removed from cup.

To measure confectioners sugar: If necessary, sift sugar to remove any lumps. Spoon lightly into nested measuring cup and level top of cup with knife.

To measure shortening or peanut butter: Pack firmly into nested measuring cup and level top of cup with knife.

To measure liquids: Use a liquid measuring cup placed on a flat surface. Pour ingredient into cup and check measuring line at eye level.

To measure honey or syrup: For more accurate measurement, lightly spray measuring cup or spoon with cooking spray before measuring so the liquid will release easily from cup or spoon.

To measure dry ingredients equaling less than ¼ cup: Dip measuring spoon into ingredient and level top of spoon with knife.

TESTS FOR CANDY MAKING

There are 2 ways to determine the correct temperature of cooked candy. The first is to use a candy thermometer. To check the accuracy of a candy thermometer, place it in a small saucepan of water over high heat and bring to a boil. Thermometer should register 212 degrees when water boils. If it does not, adjust the temperature range for each candy consistency accordingly. Insert thermometer into mixture, making sure thermometer does not touch bottom or sides of pan.

The second method to determine the correct temperature of cooked candy is the cold water test. Remove pan from heat and drop about ½ teaspoon of candy mixture into a cup of ice water. Use a fresh cup of water for each test. Use the following descriptions to determine if candy has reached the correct consistency:

Soft Ball Stage (234 to 240 degrees): candy can be rolled into a soft ball in ice water but will flatten when held in your hand.

Firm Ball Stage (242 to 248 degrees): candy can be rolled into a firm ball in ice water but will flatten if pressed when removed from the water.

Hard Ball Stage (250 to 268 degrees): candy can be rolled into a hard ball in ice water and will remain hard when removed from the water.

Soft Crack Stage (270 to 290 degrees): candy will form hard threads in ice water but will soften when removed from the water.

Hard Crack Stage (300 to 310 degrees): candy will form brittle threads in ice water and will remain brittle when removed from the water.

SEALING JARS

To seal jars, wash and dry jars, lids, and screw rings. Place jars on a rack in a large Dutch oven. Place lids in a saucepan; cover jars and lids with water. Bring both pans to a boil; boil 10 minutes. Drain and dry jars and lids completely before filling. Fill jars to within ¼ inch of tops. Wipe jar rims and threads. Quickly cover with lids and screw rings on tightly. If using a decorative lid insert, place insert into screw ring and screw in place over flat part of lid. Invert jars 5 minutes; turn upright. Sealed jars must be refrigerated.

SEALING WITH PARAFFIN

Caution: Do not melt paraffin over an open flame or directly on burner.

Melt paraffin in a double boiler over hot water. If desired, use small pieces of crayon to tint paraffin. Carefully pour a ⅛-inch thick layer of paraffin into filled food container. Allow paraffin to harden. Sealed containers must be refrigerated.

SOFTENING BUTTER

To soften butter or margarine, remove wrapper from butter and place on a microwave-safe plate. Microwave 1 stick 20 to 30 seconds at medium-low (30%).

SOFTENING CREAM CHEESE

To soften cream cheese, remove wrapper from cream cheese and place on a microwave-safe plate. Microwave 1 to 1½ minutes at medium (50%) for one 8-ounce package or 30 to 45 seconds for one 3-ounce package.

SUBSTITUTING HERBS

To substitute fresh herbs for dried, use 1 tablespoon fresh chopped herbs for ½ teaspoon dried herbs.

WHIPPING CREAM

For greatest volume, chill bowl, beaters, and cream 1 hour before whipping. In warm weather, place chilled bowl over ice while whipping cream.

BEATING EGG WHITES

For greatest volume, beat egg whites at room temperature in a clean, dry metal or glass bowl.

MELTING CHOCOLATE OR ALMOND BARK

To melt chocolate, place chopped or shaved chocolate in top of a double boiler (or in a bowl over a saucepan of water) over hot, not boiling water. Stir occasionally until melted. Remove from heat and use chocolate for dipping as desired. If necessary, chocolate may be returned to heat to remelt.

CUTTING COOKIE SHAPES

To cut out cookie shapes, dip cookie or biscuit cutter in water to keep dough from sticking to cutter.

GRATING CHEESE

To grate cheese easily, place wrapped cheese in freezer for 10 to 20 minutes before grating.

EQUIVALENT MEASUREMENTS

1 tablespoon	=	3 teaspoons
⅛ cup (1 fluid ounce)	=	2 tablespoons
¼ cup (2 fluid ounces)	=	4 tablespoons
⅓ cup	=	5⅓ tablespoons
½ cup (4 fluid ounces)	=	8 tablespoons
¾ cup (6 fluid ounces)	=	12 tablespoons
1 cup (8 fluid ounces)	=	16 tablespoons or ½ pint
2 cups (16 fluid ounces)	=	1 pint
1 quart (32 fluid ounces)	=	2 pints
½ gallon (64 fluid ounces)	=	2 quarts
1 gallon (128 fluid ounces)	=	4 quarts

HELPFUL FOOD EQUIVALENTS

½ cup butter	=	1 stick butter
1 square baking chocolate	=	1 ounce chocolate
6 ounces chocolate chips	=	1 cup chocolate chips
2¼ cups packed brown sugar	=	1 pound brown sugar
3½ cups confectioners sugar	=	1 pound confectioners sugar
2 cups granulated sugar	=	1 pound granulated sugar
4 cups all-purpose flour	=	1 pound all-purpose flour
1 cup grated cheese	=	4 ounces cheese
3 cups sliced carrots	=	1 pound carrots
½ cup sliced celery	=	1 rib celery
½ cup chopped onion	=	1 medium onion
1 cup chopped green pepper	=	1 large green pepper

General Instructions

TRANSFERRING PATTERNS

When entire pattern is shown, place a piece of tracing paper over pattern and trace pattern, marking all placement symbols and markings. Cut out traced pattern.

When one-half of pattern is shown, fold tracing paper in half and place fold along dashed line of pattern. Trace pattern half, marking all placement symbols and markings; turn folded paper over and draw over all markings. Cut out traced pattern; unfold pattern and lay it flat.

SEWING SHAPES

1. Center pattern on wrong side of 1 fabric piece and use a fabric marking pencil to draw around pattern. DO NOT CUT OUT SHAPE.
2. Place fabric pieces right sides together. Leaving an opening for turning, carefully sew pieces together directly on pencil line.
3. Leaving a $\frac{1}{4}''$ seam allowance, cut out shape. Clip seam allowance at curves and corners. Turn shape right side out. Use the rounded end of a small crochet hook to completely turn small areas.
4. If pattern has facial features or detail lines, use fabric marking pencil to lightly mark placement of features or lines.

HOW TO STENCIL

1. Trace pattern onto tracing paper. Use transfer paper to transfer design to center of tagboard. Use craft knife to cut out stencil.
2. (*Note:* Use removable tape to mask any cutout areas on stencil next to area being painted.) Hold or tape stencil in place. Use a clean dry stencil brush for each color of paint. Dip brush in paint and remove excess paint on a paper towel. Brush should be almost dry to produce good results. Beginning at edge of cutout area, apply paint in a stamping motion. If desired, shade design by stamping additional paint around edge of cutout area. Carefully remove stencil and allow paint to dry.

PAPIER MÂCHÉ

1. Follow manufacturer's instructions to mix instant papier mâché with water. Excess mixture can be stored in a resealable plastic bag in refrigerator for up to 4 days.
2. Use measurements given in project instructions as general guidelines. Keep fingers wet when working with papier mâché. Apply a $\frac{1}{8}''$ to $\frac{1}{4}''$ thick layer of papier mâché over indicated shape(s). If indicated, follow project instructions to add additional details to wet papier mâché. Allow to dry completely before applying gesso.

SEALING BOTTLE WITH WAX

You will need paraffin, 20" of cotton string, double boiler or electric frying pan and a metal can for melting paraffin, pieces of crayon with paper removed (to color paraffin), masking tape, and newspaper.

Caution: Do not melt paraffin over an open flame or directly on burner.

1. Cover work area with newspaper. Melt paraffin to a depth of $2\frac{1}{2}''$ in double boiler over hot water or in a can placed in an electric frying pan filled with water. Add pieces of crayon to melted paraffin until desired color is achieved.
2. (*Note:* Make sure cork is firmly inserted in bottle or cap is screwed on tightly.) On neck of bottle, center string on front; bring string around bottle to back and twist lengths tightly together (Fig. 1a). Keeping string taut, bring both ends over top of bottle (Fig. 1b); tape ends to front of bottle 4" below top.

Fig. 1a

Fig. 1b

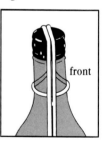

3. Dip approximately 2" of top of bottle in melted paraffin. Allowing paraffin to harden slightly between coats, continue dipping bottle until string is well coated. Remove tape; trim ends of string.
4. To open bottle, pull string up toward top of bottle and unwrap string around bottle, breaking wax.

FABRIC BAG

1. To determine width of fabric needed, add $\frac{1}{2}''$ to finished width of bag; to determine length of fabric needed, double the finished height of bag and add $1\frac{1}{2}''$. Cut fabric the determined width and length.

2. With right sides together and matching short edges, fold fabric in half; finger press folded edge (bottom of bag). Using a $\frac{1}{4}''$ seam allowance and thread to match fabric, sew sides of bag together.

3. Press top edge of bag $\frac{1}{4}''$ to wrong side; press $\frac{1}{2}''$ to wrong side again and stitch in place.

4. For bag with a flat bottom, match each side seam to fold line at bottom of bag; sew across each corner $1''$ from end (Fig. 1). Turn bag right side out.

Fig. 1

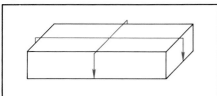

GIFT BOX 1

Note: Use this technique to cover square or rectangular cardboard boxes that are already assembled such as shoe boxes, department store gift boxes, or some candy boxes.

1. For box lid, refer to Fig. 1 to measure length and width of lid (including sides). Add $1\frac{1}{2}''$ to each measurement; cut wrapping paper the determined size.

Fig. 1

2. Place wrapping paper right side down on a flat surface; center box lid, top side down, on paper. For 1 short side of box lid, cut paper diagonally from corners to within $\frac{1}{16}''$ of box (Fig. 2). Fold short edge of paper up and over side of lid (Fig. 3); crease paper along folds and tape edge in place inside lid. Repeat for remaining short side.

Fig. 2

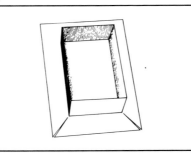

Fig. 3

3. For 1 long side of box lid, fold edges of paper as shown in Fig. 4; crease paper along folds. Fold paper up and over side of lid; crease paper along folds

and tape edge in place inside lid. Repeat for remaining long side.

Fig. 4

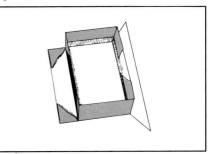

4. Repeat Steps 1 - 3 for bottom of box.

GIFT BOX 2

Note: Use this technique to cover cardboard boxes that are unassembled or are easily unfolded such as cake boxes.

1. Place wrapping paper right side down on a flat surface. Unfold box to be covered.

2. For a small box, apply spray adhesive to outside of entire box. Place box, adhesive side down, on paper; press firmly to secure.

3. For a large box, apply spray adhesive to bottom of box. Center box, adhesive side down, on paper; press firmly to secure. Applying spray adhesive to 1 section at a time, repeat to secure remaining sections of box to paper.

4. Use a craft knife to cut paper even with edges of box. If box has slits, use craft knife to cut through slits from inside of box.

5. Reassemble box.

Continued on page 124

GENERAL INSTRUCTIONS (continued)

CROSS STITCH

COUNTED CROSS STITCH

Work 1 Cross Stitch to correspond to each colored square on the chart. For horizontal rows, work stitches in 2 journeys (Fig. 1). For vertical rows, complete each stitch as shown in Fig. 2. When the chart shows a Backstitch crossing a colored square (Fig. 3), a Cross Stitch (Fig. 1 or 2) should be worked first; then the Backstitch (Fig. 5) should be worked on top of the Cross Stitch.

Fig. 1

Fig. 2

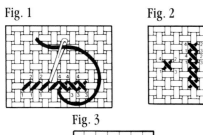

Fig. 3

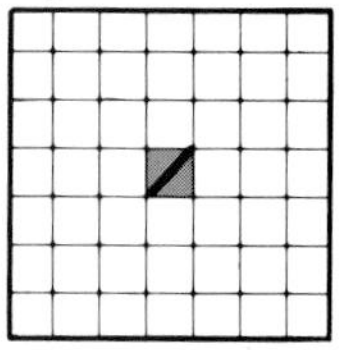

QUARTER STITCH (¼X)

Quarter Stitches are denoted by triangular shapes of color on the chart and on the color key. Come up at 1 (Fig. 4); then split fabric thread to go down at 2.

Fig. 4

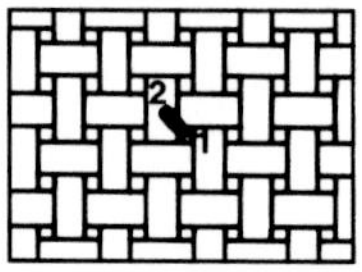

BACKSTITCH

For outline detail, Backstitch (shown on chart and on color key by black or colored straight lines) should be worked after the design has been completed (Fig. 5).

Fig. 5

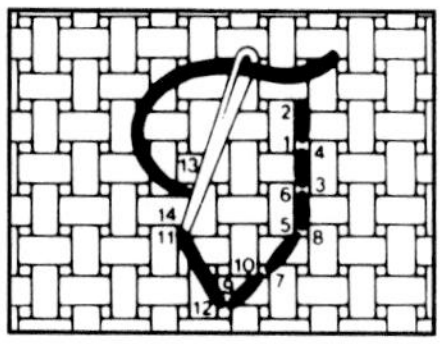

FRENCH KNOT

Bring needle up at 1. Wrap thread once around needle and insert needle at 2, holding end of thread with non-stitching fingers (Fig. 6). Tighten knot; then pull needle through fabric, holding thread until it must be released. For a larger knot, use more strands; wrap only once.

Fig. 6

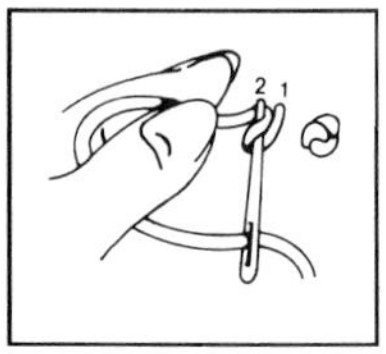

CREDITS

To Magna IV Engravers of Little Rock, Arkansas, we say thank you for the superb color reproduction and excellent pre-press preparation.

We want to especially thank photographers Mark Mathews and Ken West of Peerless Photography, Little Rock, Arkansas, for their time, patience, and excellent work.

To the talented people who helped in the creation of some of the projects in this book, we extend a special word of thanks.

Santa Mug, page 43: Diane Brakefield
Bread Cloth, page 87: Ann Townsend
Holiday Apron, page 111: Lorraine Birmingham
Joy Ornament, page 117: Mary Beach Jones

We extend a sincere thank you to the people who assisted in making and testing the projects and recipes in this book: Mary Carlton, Joan Taylor Cunningham, and Nelda Newby.

RECIPE INDEX

C

A

B

THE SPIRIT OF CHRISTMAS
BOOK FIVE

Ooohs, Aaahs, & Mmms
GUARANTEED!

Make this Christmas a memory they'll always cherish with *The Spirit of Christmas* from Leisure Arts. Filled with more than 160 all-new projects and recipes, this luxurious volume will lead you step-by-step through decorating your home and tree, cooking and baking for all your festive gatherings, and gift-making for everyone on your list.

- 160 Joy-filled pages
- Lavish photographs
- Easy, clear instructions

To review *The Spirit of Christmas* in your home free for 21 days, call the toll-free number on this page or write to Leisure Arts, P.O. Box 10576, Des Moines, IA 50340-0576. If you're delighted with our book, pay just $19.95 (in U.S. funds), plus postage and handling. (In Canadian funds, $26.00 plus postage and handling; a 7% goods and services tax applies to all Canadian orders.) If not completely delighted, you may return the book within 21 days and owe nothing. If you keep it, you are eligible to receive future annuals *on approval*. You are in no way obligated to buy future books, and you may cancel at any time just by notifying us. Please allow 6-8 weeks for delivery. Limited time offer.

Also available at your local needlecraft shop!

FREE FOR 21 DAYS
CALL TOLL FREE 1-800-666-6326

More!

glorious gifts to cook and craft!

Create a lasting impression with the delicious projects in *Gifts of Good Taste* and *Gifts That Taste Good*. Inside these unique volumes from Leisure Arts' popular Memories in the Making series, you'll find a winning combination: scrumptious homemade goodies and imaginative packaging ideas for every occasion! Add these two companion volumes to *Christmas Gifts of Good Taste* for a terrific trio of gift-idea books.

- Over 200 creative ideas
- Delicious, easy recipes
- Beautiful (and simple) handmade crafts
- Colorful photographs
- Clear, concise instructions

To order these indispensable volumes, send $18.95 (in U.S. funds) plus $1.95 postage and handling for each book to Memories in the Making, P.O. Box 10108, Des Moines, IA 50340-0108. (In Canadian funds, $26.00 plus $1.95 postage and handling for each book. A 7% goods and services tax applies to all Canadian orders.) Please allow 6-8 weeks for delivery. Limited time offer.

CALL TOLL-FREE
1-800-288-8990
(Visa or MasterCard orders only)

Also available at your local needlecraft shop!